The Golden Tr(age)dy

Shannon Craig

Write hard and clear about what
hurts.

-Ernest Hemingway

Part One

Let me tell you a story about myself. The experiences through my eyes, the people through my lips, and the feelings through my heart. Let me extend my hand to you, widen your eyes for me, open your ears to me. See, it was December, and I have this nasty and peculiar habit of reading outside when it's cold. I had convinced myself that books always seemed more real if you read them outside. And honestly, I read my books like I read my music; with an odd amount of passion. But there I was, curled up on my front porch in the snow. My lips were blue and my hands were numb and I didn't care. I was reading a book that was completely composed of free verse poems. I have this horrible fascination with poetry and I suppose you could call me a poet just like how you could call me a musician. But the thing is, I looked up from my book. This never happens. Maybe once, or even twice, when all of the planets are aligned or something to that effect- but it's a rarity. But I looked up and saw this tall, lanky, awkward guy walking down my street. He was dressed in all black which was a stark contrast with the paleness of his skin and the purity of the snow. I was so fascinated by the way he walked, he took long, loping strides. It was the type of walk that made you want to just spend hours listening to what he had to say. You didn't even know what it was exactly that he had to say, but you knew it was something good.

We locked eyes and he smiled as if I was some long lost childhood friend. I remember that smile, I remember feeling panicky because it was such a familiar smile that I thought I had met him before. I suppose one thing led to another and my legs decided it was a good idea to walk me over to him. I'm still debating to this day whether or not that was a good idea. Now, I wasn't much of a talker, I'm still not, but I've made some pretty great progress. Well, I

guess you could call it great,
I'm still debating about this as
well. See back then, I would go
weeks without speaking. I made a
vow to myself that I would never
say anything if people were
simply listening. Which happens a
lot because people tend to listen
to things, but they'll never hear
them. Which is disappointing. But
I offered him the best that I
could, I gave him a muffled hello
which was slightly hushed because
my voice didn't really get much
use, but what can I say. Come to
think of it, all he did was

smile. He never said hello back. He simply took my hand and gestured for me to walk with him. Suddenly, free verse poetry books weren't so interesting anymore. I remember as he was leading me through the winding streets of my neighborhood, I was thinking about how I had stopped reading. How I had simply looked up from the story of the lives I thought I would never lead, how my eyes had strayed away from the words I simply did not have the courage to speak. It was so odd though, we were walking through the streets I had walked through hundreds of times before, so why was it that this felt like the first time I had stepped outside? Why was it, that the air felt so cold and crisp? The sun so bright? Every sound so clear? He had brought me to this forgotten trail that led into some woods. I like to think that I'm pretty well versed on the subject of the five mile radius around my house, but this path I had never seen before. The trees stood so tall, so strong, like a bunch of guards. You could feel this sacred secret caressing your mind, like a wise voice whispering in your ear. As we were walking through this gentle wonderland, he began to speak to me.

Passing through all the trees, I remember comparing his voice to the snow on the branches. So solid, yet so fragile all at the same time. Looking at his long, skinny limbs, he reminded me of a rejected Tim Burton character. I had noticed that he always kept his lips slightly parted. I never figured out if life was flowing into him, or out. He looked down at me, taking in my details, as I was to him. Staring at me intently, he began, "I don't know how to go about saying this. So I figured we'd just slam it down on the table so everything won't seem so tacky and cliche. I've been roaming around the Pennsylvania/Ohio area since last May. My parents died and so I ran. I'm trying to get to Chicago but I knew I had to find something. You can tell me this is creepy, but you have to be that something. There is this wisdom to you and it fascinates me. I need to spend time with you, I want to know everything about you."

His brute honestly shocked me, but reminded me of myself. Terribly. I nodded. It honestly felt like everything was staged, I felt like I was on the outside looking in. These things don't just happen, you know? This is what lonely people like myself write books about. It was like

stumbling across a B flat and a C
Sharp at the same time in a piece
of music, it's weird, but there
it is just sitting on the page,
staring at you. You can almost
hear it whispering, yes I exist,
please play me. It was like that.
Life was sitting there telling
me, yes I'm real, take the
opportunity or forever wish you
had. After an inappropriate
length of silence on my end, I
looked his in the eyes and asked
when we'd be leaving. He told me
within the month.

See, I was still in school at this time. And I was sort of passionate about that, too. Because I have this crazy fantasy that I'm going to graduate high school and get accepted into the College of Berkeley in California (no, the school is not 'radical' anymore. Please, for gods sake, get with the times. Thank you.) So I'd road trip it across the country and meet dozens of wonderfully fascinating people along the way, become enlightened, and continue on with my life. But I sort of needed to

graduate before all of this
happened. So no running away to
Chicago with strange boys for me.
I told him we had a two week
break around Christmas. He smiled
and told me he'd love to spend
Christmas with me.

Well, okay.

So we both sat there. Him,
excited about actually finding
the something. Me, stressing out
over the fact that this actually
real life. Was this part of my
Golden Tragedy? See, a Golden

Tragedy was a phrase I had become somewhat infatuated with. If you look closely, you can see that the word age is within the word tragedy. A golden age is a time of happiness, prosper, knowledge, and whatever else. So, in my eyes, every person has one of these and it comes out of a tragedy in a person's life, thus why the word age is in the middle of the word tragedy. Coincidence? I beg to differ. If I had learned anything, ever, from being such an observer it was that. That living is not simply being alive

and that everyone has a Golden
Tragedy. I'm convinced this was
mine. Sitting there with him in
the snow, I trusted someone for
the first time in my life. It was
terrifying.

So once again, we walked in
silence. He held my arm because I
was shaking. From nerves, from
cold, I could not tell you. Maybe
a little bit of both? I gave him
my phone number. He smiled at the
paper and said he'd find a
perfect stranger and call me with
that phone so we could devise our

Golden Tragedy . See, at this point, I had explained to him what a Golden Tragedy was because he heard me muttering about it so I sort of had to. That's another habit of mine, muttering to myself. God, gotta stop doing that. So we turned and went our separate ways. Me, into the warmth of my home and him back down the street, turning back towards the way he had so mysteriously came from. A few days passed and I was mostly frustrated with everything because I was frustrated about waiting. The only happy thing that happened, was with this little autistic boy that I help with his school work. See, he had wanted to bake muffins for his teacher so I helped him make cranberry ones. Once we were done, he suddenly remembered she had said she hated cranberries. So I stayed with him in till 1 AM on a Wednesday, making blueberry muffins. I suppose this should have pissed me off more, but I have a soft spot for him. However, on the 5th day, he called.

I told him how I was supposed to go to my Aunt's for Christmas. It hadn't occurred to me the first time I saw him, but she lived in Chicago. I was completely convinced that me going to Chicago with him was manifest destiny. I was going to achieve my Golden Tragedy and become enlightened. We agreed that we'd meet at the airport at promptly 8 o'clock at night, when my flight landed. I called my aunt to tell her I'd be spending the holidays at a friends. She was thrilled because she didn't like me too much anyway. Another example of the manifest destiny I suppose. I had exactly 11 days before I was to be seeing him. They were filled with pacing, writing, doubting, and everything else that stresses me out. I kept waiting for someone to realize what was going on, but no one ever did. Another hidden talent of mine is being ignorable though. All of those speeches that you get in elementary school about how there's bad people in the world everywhere nipped at

the back of my mind, but in the
end I would disregard it.

I was going to Chicago
tomorrow.

I had packed and everything.
I had money for the 10 days I
would be spending there. I was
nervous and excited and scared
all at the same time. But above
all, I remember that I was ready.
This town wanted nothing to do
with me. I was an outcast and I
knew it. The burden of my broken
family suffocated me and I had

given up on gluing the parts back
together. My father could not
tell you the first thing about me
and my mother would just make it
up. My sister had ran away a bit
over a year ago and I hadn't
heard from her since. As hard as
it was to accept, she was dead to
me. But looking back on it, I
hadn't accepted that. I still
cried over her.

See, growing up, we had
depended on each other. She made
me the individual that I am
today. Now, whether that was more

influenced by her or the lack of,
I could not tell you. But to put
it frankly, I needed her and she
needed me. We offered each other
what little comfort that could be
had amongst the broken glass that
had become my family. To this
day, I'm still trying to figure
out what exactly a family is. So
far, I've concluded that it is
complete and utter bullshit, but
I've been challenging myself to
prove that wrong. On a personal
level, we all don't love each
other; we just live together.
Countless nights of being deemed

a disappointment and being messed with on a psychological level that will have you doubting yourself constantly for the rest of your life, sort of ripped our family portrait in half.

Since then, I had created an alter-ego for myself; one to present to my family. It was a satisfactory picture for them, and kept them distanced from me. Call it pathetic, call it a defense mechanism, I don't care. They don't see things the way I do, so I've created a few optical illusions. They figured out that I write poetry, they've just never read it. My mom tried to read one of my poems once and I took it out of her hand and ripped it into an accurate representation of the words on that page. Destroyed. She doesn't try to read my poems anymore. They might be catching on that I'm into music, but I think it's more along the lines of 'oh, she think's it'll look good on college applications so that's why she spends so much time on it'. Not an actual passion, not an actual thing that someone would need like oxygen. In their eyes, it is a thing, a hobby. And that's how it should be because it matches the picture I've painted for them. But the thing they'll never figure out is that the picture is a puzzle, each piece containing an ounce of what I am. No less, no more. I somehow managed to reason that since we have similar DNA, I shouldn't be a complete liar. Just mostly. Because if DNA meant anything, we wouldn't keep our distant family in cages, now would we? Food for thought I suppose.

But there I was, standing
wide-eyed in the airport and he
came to me, open armed. I
remember feeling like I belonged
for the first time in my life,
it's funny because this should be
something that should feel so
dangerous, so foreign, but I
belonged. And maybe that's what I
had been searching for this
entire time, what I'm still
looking for. We walked down empty
alleys as he led me through the

dumping land of the city. I've decided that if Chicago was a person, it'd be a women. Let me tell you, she is a bitch, she is a whore, and she is so beautiful. The neon lights enticed me, the people fascinated me, the snow was a blanket, acting like makeup, covering up all the lines that she was self conscious about seeing. In my eyes, she was perfect.

He brought me to this little apartment building and looking back at it, I don't know if anyone else lived there because I never saw anyone. We put my bag in a room that was very brown and stereotypical. I imagined that the walls had turned from white to brown from all the secrets they had absorbed. I've always wondered what walls would say if they could speak. We still hadn't spoken to each other. He opened the window, letting in the harsh winter air and gestured for me to follow him out on the fire escape. He explained to me that he had a job, working with a photographer and that he had talked to him about me and that he wanted to take pictures of me. I'd never thought of myself as beautiful, quirky perhaps, but never beautiful. Telling this to him, he simply replied that I wasn't beautiful, I was art. Looking out at the sky, I realized I could not see the stars. We shared a bed that night, we kept to our separate sides. Whispering in the dark, he told me his name was Jack. Repeating it back to him, I liked how it felt on my lips; safe.

This was the first time I had slept in three days.

The next morning, I woke to find him outside of the fire escape. I went into the small bathroom, which I noticed was the only other room in the tiny apartment. Turning on the shower, I figured out that the warm water would never come so I took my first frigid shower. I can't take hot ones anymore because it stresses me out. Feeling the cold water on my skin, I could think clearly. I started to take in

what I was doing. I would be
lying if I didn't tell you I was
scared. Not of him, but of
everything else. I was in a bad
part of a city I wasn't terribly
familiar with, in an apartment
with a guy I had just learned the
name of hours before. God damn.
Despite my realization of where I
was, I managed to pull my clothes
on, put some makeup on, and walk
out the door with him into a
world much different than the
comfort and warmth of the
apartment. He led me confidently
through the streets as I took in

the world around me. Everyone looked like they had a purpose, even the homeless people knew what they were doing. I felt like a kid riding a bike for the first time, I was aware that I was going to fall on my face eventually, but I enjoyed the accomplishment of actually riding the bike while I could. We quickly turned into an airy building with extremely bright lighting. A voice chirped from the back room, asking if that was Jack. Smiling, he announced that he had brought *the girl.*

Blushing, I shook the man's hand who introduced himself to me as Derek. Pulling at my jacket and my hand, he led me to the back room and sat me in front of a mirror and set to work. With eyes painted black and lips painted red, I stood in front of a camera for the first time. See, Derek was a photographer, and a fairly successful one. Claiming me as his muse for his new collection, he told me to appear angry and beautiful at the same time. Taking on the role of someone I had never met, my face conveying feelings I was not terribly familiar with, I became her. After a few hours, Derek peered over his camera at me and grinned. "Darling, you will be famous and you will be fabulous." Staring down at the expensive looking navy dress I was wearing, I believed him.

Muttering about how he didn't want to waste my appearance by hiding it from the world, Derek invited Jack and I to a party he was attending. Jack and I had confessed we had never

been to a true party, but
reluctantly agreed, both enticed
by the evening's opportunity.
Managing to get a cab with
graceful ease, Derek told the
driver the address in a hushed
tone. The driver winked at me. As
we raced through the winding
streets, I stared out the window,
taking in the beauty of the city.
Looking up at the buildings, the
skyscrapers looked as if they
broke through the atmosphere,
like their top floors were
reaching for the moon. If you
looked long enough, you could

believe that the tallest ones had touched it before. We stopped abruptly and Derek climbed out, holding the door like a gentleman. My bare legs were met by the frigid air and I shivered as we quickly walked down a flight of stairs to a door that led into the club. Music blared loudly and Jack held my hand as we were led into the main room. Hundreds of bodies flung themselves around in such a fashion, you would have thought their lives depended on the degree of their dancing. I wanted so desperately to be a part of it. Dozens of people flocked Derek, all asking about his guests. I smiled prettily at everyone, shaking hands and eventually being led of to the dancing. A tall, dark, and handsome stranger offered me his flask, claiming it would calm the nerves. A calming of the nerves was a rarity, so I took a swig. The liquid burned my throat and after a few more swigs, my head became fuzzy. I could feel the music pulsing through me as I participated in the ritual of dancing.

A strange bond was made
between me and everyone around
me. We acted and reacted to each
other, touching, grabbing, and
teasing each other. Shimmying in
perfect time, we were transformed
into something so tragic and so
beautiful. The hours felt like
minutes and I had lost sight of
Jack. Derek sat in a booth,
smiling knowingly at the scene on
the dancefloor. A girl I had not
seen before took my hand and led
me towards a door. Pulling me

into the bathroom, her and her
friends smiled at me and
introduced themselves since it
was apparent they already knew
me. They asked if I was new to
the industry. The reluctance in
my response gave them their
answer. They sharpened their
nails while I bit my cuticles.
Quickly, they decided to deem me
an 'absolute doll'. I studied
their thin legs, long fingers,
and small frames. Glancing down
at myself, I decided I had found
my 'thinspiration'. Painting the
area around my eyes a darker

shade of black, we strutted back
onto the dance floor like we were
untouchable. I blended in
perfectly, as if this is where I
came every night of my life. No
one would have thought that I had
never done this. I was a doll, a
canvas, paint me as you please. I
don't know how much time passed,
but Jack's hand found mine
through a mass of bodies and he
gently led me out of the packed
building.

Grinning at each other, we
hailed a cab and shared our

silent secret of the night's events. We ran up the steps of the apartment building and quickly slid out onto the fire escape. He stared at me and told me I reminded him of a celebrity and that he thought I was a miracle. He said he was paid $200 for being my escort. The oddity of the statement set me aback, I asked him to explain the concept. Looking down at his hands he told me that in the 'society', men sat in booths and paid escorts for bringing them something to watch. It had not occurred to me that I was being watched, that the people that spoke to me were the same ones talking about me in the booths. He explained that Derek got great feedback about me and that he wanted to take me again in two days time. It was easy money and I had a fascination with the sinful atmosphere so I agreed. Looking out at the rising sun, I asked what time it was. Jack told me it was 8 AM. Realizing that we had spent about 7 hours at the club, we climbed into bed and slept in till nightfall.

It was about 6 PM when I woke up, only to find Jack packing a bag getting ready to head out the door. He smiled and me and told me good morning. Asking where he was going, he told me he had to go to work and that he'd be back in the morning. The realization that I had the night to myself crept upon me. I got up quickly after he left, making haste to get out the door. The thrill of freedom caressed my bones, bringing goosebumps to my skin. The night was young and I felt on top of the world. Sneaking into a friendly looking bookstore, I had found my happiness. The smell of unopened pages, the excitement of unread words, flooded me. Brushing my fingertips over the spines of the books, I couldn't help but grin. I stared intently at the titles, deciding which one to claim as my victim first. It was truly perfection except my fascination had gotten the best to me, and I slammed into an unsuspecting body. We both immediately exploded with apologies, nervously stuttering, and finally locking eyes. Our hands had been touching the same book. Pulling away, I apologized for about the million and a halfth time. A grin crept across his face, one that I will never forget. The image of his smile slowly revealing itself to me has been forever burned into my mind. He asked if I had read the book and asked if I would read it with him. My heart didn't skip a beat, let me tell you, it had completely stopped. We huddled together in a booth and poured over the words.

Whispering the story to each
other, we didn't stop until we
had taken in every letter, cover
to cover. When it was over, he
stared at me. It wasn't a shy
glance, he blatantly stared into
my eyes and told me I was
ravishing. Blushing furiously, I
took his hand as he walked me
back to my apartment. When we got
to the front of the building, he
kissed my forehead, promising to
see me again. As I opened the
door, I turned back and looked at
him again, only to see he was
doing the exact same thing. His

name was Kevin and he reminded me
of a promise. I realized today
was Christmas.

It turned out that I had
gotten home before Jack, but the
sun was beginning to rise. I
drifted off into a simple
slumber, only waking up when he
got back. Climbing in next to me,
we slept in till nightfall once
again. However, we were disturbed
by knocking on the door. It was
Derek, when we answered he smiled
and bustled in. Herding me into
the small bathroom, he set to

work. Pinching and fixing and perfecting, I turned towards the mirror looking like a different person. He gave me heels and another dress. With that, we set out into the night. Hailing a cab with the same remarkable speed, we set off to the same destination. The club felt familiar once we arrived, and we were immediately greeted by dozens of people. We parted ways fairly quickly, me towards the dance floor, Derek and Jack to the booths. The thought of people watching me dance nipped at the back of my mind, but the same warm liquid I drank the other night shushed the worries. And so I danced. I danced as if it was all I knew how to do. Hands pawed at me, touching me, brushing me. A couple hours later, I was exhausted. A friendly voice whispered in my ear, a calloused hand offered me brightly colored pills. Common sense was fogged by fatigue, so I swallowed two. Ecstasy was eventually going to blossom into my drug of choice. Everything felt so bright and promising, I was in love with

everything and everyone. I felt
beautiful and shiny as I danced
with a renewed passion. Once
again, time had began to lapse
and the hours turned to minutes,
minutes into seconds. Every
sensation was so real, so
enhanced. Every touch was a
promise, every person a gift. I
was in that club for three days.
Honestly, I don't remember much.
I would pass out and regain
consciousness and take another
pill. The music never stopped, so
neither did we. Food and water
was sort of passed around to

everyone, we took it like it was
a gift from God. But we never
stopped dancing.

I don't know how he found
me, but Jack took my hand and
once again led me towards the
door. I mumbled something
incoherently, smiling at him like
he was an old friend. I don't
know what he was on, or what he
wasn't, but he smiled back.
Except the smile didn't reach his
eyes. His eyes remained the same,
so empty, so tired. I didn't ask
him what he was paid because I

could tell he was ashamed. But
I'd do it for him, I'd do
anything for him and that was the
sin of it. I liked him too much.
And I couldn't tell you how we
got back to the apartment, but I
slept. I slept like it was what I
was made to do. Jack would wake
me to give me food and water, but
that was it. The dreams I had
were vivid and terrifying. I'd
really rather not tell you about
those. I still wake up crying
from them today. But I'd rather
not tell you about that either.
But slowly I regained my sanity.

My time in Chicago had ended. My
flight was that evening. Packing
my bags, I mulled over the entire
experience. I realized I couldn't
remember the majority of it. So
Jack and I walked in comfortable
silence to the airport. He hugged
me awkwardly, and told me he'd
call. We had planned for me to
come back in March.

As the plane took off, I
closed my eyes and I wept. I wept
for my experience, I wept for my
misery, I wept for how I was
addicted to it all. And so the

plane landed and I returned to my quiet lifestyle. It was so surreal, just jumping back into it like that. I had three months to think about those few days. More than anything, I thought of Kevin. And how I hadn't seen him after that day. Tell me, why is it that the person I saw for the least amount of time, has the most effect on me? It's like he was searching for my heart, but so far all he had found was the electric fencing and barbed wire that I surround it with. Tell me, why is it that I am already agreeing to throwing in the key and taking it all down for a perfect stranger? I'll tell you. Because love is not logical. I'm telling you now that there is nothing logical about putting the most fragile parts of you in hands that tremble and shake. Let me offer you what little wisdom I possess- they will be dropped. But like any good story, I have to include details. The months that I was home were not entirely uneventful. See, this is when I met Ana. Now, some of you know what I'm talking about. Just like how some of you understand when I tell you that all of our pencil sharpeners were suddenly missing a piece. Because I got home and I was skin and bone. I was fragile and I was on the verge of breaking. Over the next few months I would test how far I could take my body without destroying it. I was 27 pounds underweight when I went back in March. Scars decorated my wrists and vodka stained my breath. Oh, I had changed. Was it because of love, or lack of? It was a lust that I felt for the city, a need

I felt for him.

I found my way back to the
city, the way that cold air seems
to find a way back through a
draft you thought you fixed
months ago. No matter how many
times I thought to myself, *maybe
this is a bad idea,* the sinful
temptation found a way into my
every thought. It was like the
simple idea of it was breathing
down my neck, reflecting itself
in my every move. Entering the
apartment, it never more felt
like a refuge. That feeling of

belonging had returned once more.
Jack and I met eyes as I entered
and we shared the same smile.
Dropping my bags on the floor, I
took his hand and we became once
more, creatures of the night.

Going down those same stairs
was so surreal. It was like being
led to your execution except for
you were suicidal. I'm telling
you, I took the pills. I walked
through the shadow of death. I
was shaking so much it had felt
as if everything was still. I was
on the outside looking in, a mere

bystander for the destruction of
my own self. So I prayed to a God
I wasn't sure I believed in,
scraped my already cut up knees,
and bit the apple out of fear. I
gave into it all. I was done
fighting for a life I wasn't sure
I was ready to live. But there
was something in me, that told me
to leave. So there I was,
wandering aimlessly around the
streets of Chicago , squinting at
the daylight. I stumbled upon
that very same bookstore, and I
cried when I saw it. I held
myself the way that you would

hold an injured animal, as I
walked in, eyes down

. I had perfected the art of
being invisible, especially when
I didn't want to be seen but he
found me. He found me as if he
had been searching for me all
along and the sincerity of his
words would make you believe that
he had. For there he was, sitting
in that booth. Reading that book.
And I could almost see myself
right there beside him. He held
me with every desperation that I
had been feeling for the past 12

weeks. Every bone in my body ached for someone to love me like that. To love me as much as I loved them, for I had a terrible habit of always being the one that loved more. But there it was again, that feeling of belonging as he whispered into my hair how much he had missed me. Him kissing me was like making a promise. One that you knew you would never be able to break, that no matter what happened, I could never stop needing him. So we sat like that for three hours, holding each other. We didn't speak. There weren't words that could describe it. I memorized his hands. I could tell you how there's this vain in the middle that's slightly unproportionate with the rest of the veins because it's bigger and slightly slanted. Or how he has a scar on his left thumb because when he was a kid he tried to cut an onion and now he doesn't eat onions anymore. I could tell you how his fingertips were exactly a half inch above mine when we put our hands up against one anothers. How he'd always lean forward when he was listening to me. I could tell you everything.

Maybe we were taking things too quickly, or maybe because in the city, everything moved faster. That was the thing, everything was always progressing. Nothing ever hurt because you didn't have the time to feel it, the next thing was already presenting itself right in front of you. Maybe that's why I never saw it all coming, everything was glossed over and made shiny new again. You could

never see the flaws if you didn't
know where to look. So that was
my downfall, falling in love with
him. But I told him, I told him.
Do not pour your thoughts into me
for I am broken glass. I never
know if I am half empty or half
full. And here we are, pouring
everything we could ever hope to
have into each other. Baring our
naked souls, exposing our raw
selves. This is a connection you
can't simply disregard, these
were nights I will never cease to
forget. For the first time, I
wasn't scared. I could look him

in the eye and not be
intimidated. We were perfectly
equal. Sometimes I wondered if we
were the same person, honestly.
Ceaselessly, we buried ourselves
within each other. I was fully
immersed with every sense of his
being, I belonged to him like a
dog would to it's owner.

But I loved him.

I still have yet to decide
if he was beautifully tragic or
tragically beautiful. Let me tell
you the cold brutal truth of it.

For it's time for me to stop
lying to myself. I was taught to
fight for independance on the
back seats of cars. On stained
leather seats, I learned the true
meaning of expectations. I got
down on my knees for him when I
was 13. Because he said I would,
if I loved him. I painted myself
in what I thought were the colors
of the rainbows but it's all
really just hips and lips,
discarding clothing for a promise
that was meant to be broken. For
boundaries that were meant to be
ignored, *I shrunk away from his*

touch. I no longer blossomed from his love. No, I wilted because this so called love had affected me like frost would a flower. I wilted in till I was shriveled up in the cracks of the concrete, damned to waiting for spring to come again.

But I loved him.

I gave him everything, everything. But I heard myself say no. Over and over again, no, no, no. Why was it that when I had no words to speak, everyone

turned towards me, expecting
something? Why was it that the
one word that mattered, refused
to make a sound? *I heard myself
say no.*

But I loved him.

And maybe that's my problem,
my downfall if you will. I can't
tell people no. So maybe that's
why I continued to let my hand be
led into the spotlight. Cameras
flashing, I adored modeling
because for a few hours I could
act like the scars on my wrists

weren't from weakness, but from strength. That I was this bad ass tiger that had simply earned her stripes. I never kept any of the pictures that had been taken of me, I still see some of them floating around occasionally though. But most of them I didn't look at, I didn't want to see, to know. I hated seeing myself, I was so disgusted with the person I had become. I was skin, bones, scars, vodka, drugs, and a need for someone to approve of me. Nothing more, nothing less. It was the last night of the week I was spending in Chicago. I was supposed to go to the club and get high and dance and act like I didn't want to kill myself. But there was the impossible task of getting out the door. I stared defiantly at my own reflection. Every atom of me radiated a hatred I still struggle to describe. Fist clenched, eyes narrowed, nostrils flared, I was more disappointed than anything else. I saw imperfection. Fat, lard, everything that I wanted to cut off. I could feel my eating disorder tantalizing me, daring

me to take a knife and chop away.
The voice in my head did not tell
me to calm down. It teased my
sanity, caressing my will. *Fat.
You are so fat. You want to lose
weight? Eat in front of a mirror,
naked. Bitch.*

And so I did. I swallowed
pill after pill. Make me numb,
make me sane. I couldn't see the
way my rib cage was the widest
part of my body. I couldn't see
the way my spine protruded like a
failed attempt at keeping me
stable. I couldn't see the mile

wide gap between my thighs, representing the days I went without eating. Representing the countless nights, hunched over a god damn toilet. Hurling up everything, believing that I was becoming pure. I was a living sin, I was the living dead. Leaning over the sink, I stared into the mirror. I didn't recognize the pair of eyes that looked back.

Jack stumbled into the bathroom, the words unsaid were more crowding then his tall frame

in the room. We stared at each
other with a deep understanding.
Our eyes glazed over the surface
of the other's body. Our thoughts
were parallel to one another,
each thinking, *I need to lose
weight.* So he took my arm and I
took his hand and we finally made
it out the door.

We stumbled through the
streets like a couple of drunk
blind men, I won't even lie. But
damn, we felt so *cool.* I guess
you could blame it on the drugs,
for that's what I do everytime.

We passed all the shops and buildings that I'd seen dozens of times but this time everything was so different, so new. It was like seeing it all for the first time and being able to take it all in at once. Like standing on top of a mountain and being able to look up and down at the same time. Every window was a passage, a novel, a work of art. All having so many different secrets to whisper to me about the events inside. And I wanted so desperately to hear them all. I wanted to curl up on the sidewalk

and blend into the concrete,
comforted by the warmth of a good
story. I felt like a little kid
again, eyes lit up in wonder as
we continued down the streets. We
hadn't gotten a cab because we
wanted to go on the journey, *an
adventure.* So like the three kids
in Peter Pan, we allowed
ourselves to be swept away by it
all. We threw our hands up and
tried so hard to touch the stars.
Just a little farther..Could I
reach the stars? We giggled,
giddy, at everything we passed.
It was all so colourful and

mystical and we got the chance to be a part of it. The oh-so-familiar concrete steps that led down into the club had become a secret passage. A secret passage for a scandal only the privileged and the cool could bear the responsibility of knowing. Stepping in, I feasted on the adrenaline. Absorbing every bead of sweat, every beat of the song. Taking in the ever present scent of alcohol, drugs, and sex. This is where I learned to breathe.

As I was swept away onto the dance floor, a pair of hands quickly grabbed and gripped my bony shoulders. I laughed, pawing them away but the grip only tightened. I heard myself pleading to the hands to let me dance. That I just wanted to have *a good time*. But all I could feel was my shoulders bruising. I couldn't make out the words being growled into my ear, couldn't tell whose eyes were staring so furiously at me. But I allowed myself to be led off the

dancefloor. Allowed myself to be
led out the back door. Allowed
myself to be cornered. And not in
till then had it dawned on me
whose eyes had been watching me,
whose whisper I had heard.
Kevin's frame took over mine as
he leaned in. Closer, closer, he
came. Not stopping until we were
nose to nose, eye to eye. He
grabbed my face and yelled.
Yelled because he knew it hurt,
yelled because he knew I was
scared.

Prostitute, slut, skank,

what do you think you're doing?
You're so far out you don't even
know your own name. I'm disgusted
to be associated with you. It
disturbs me to even know your
name.

So he hit me.

They say that after the
first black eye, you should fight
back. But how can you hurt the
one you love the most? How was I
supposed to defend myself, when I
was the one who tore down my
walls for him- I let him in. I

let him tear apart my skin, I let him punch and kick and rip. I let him watch the blood spread across my skin like red wine would on a white tablecloth- I gave in. I took it all, every single ounce of his unmanageable anger. And I did it because I loved him.

He rips at my clothes, the sound of fabric separating is all I can hear. I am screaming, but there is no noise. His hands are rough, his fingers are calloused. I close my eyes. I try to push him away but he's heavy and I'm

weak and I'm scared so he hurts
me and he hurts me and he hurts
me.

But he stops, painfully
similar to that eerie calmness in
the middle of a storm. He stares
at me with wide eyes, he is
scared. Do you know what you've
done to me? I whisper, I cry. He
looks me up and down, taking in
the damage. I am shaking, I am
breaking down. I am looking up at
him, I am whispering. I am asking
him, why did you do this to me? I
can not look at him, this is not

Kevin, I do not know this man. I ask again and again, why. But he never told me. I made him angry.

There I was again, on the outside looking in. My body was screaming at me and my vision was fading anyway. So I watched myself sway, becoming more off balance with every punch he swung. I witnessed him clawing at my shoulders, oblivious to the cuts he was making, the scars he had already caused. I saw him slap me and I saw the red

handprint that had formed on my
cheek. I heard him growl,
reminding me who I belonged to. I
was a witness to my own defeat.
But though my mouth was bleeding,
though I was trembling, though my
voice was wavering, I could have
almost sworn that I heard myself
say no.

Everything was fogging up
and I couldn't feel anything. It
was as if I had already taken the
pills that I so often depended on
to make me numb. I don't remember
falling, I just remember the way

the soles of his shoes looked when he walked away. I closed my eyes and gave in. I melted into the concrete like discarded gum would on a hot summer's day, I was trash. I could hear the music coming from inside but I didn't have the strength to move. I didn't have the strength to call for help, didn't have the strength to cry. I had given up. I had let myself waver and crumble. And so I slept.

My life was falling apart and there was no denying it. I was passed out in a god damn alley

behind a club and I was dying.

And there I was, thinking about

how the bottom of his shoes

looked. I was an obscenity. Six

months ago, if you would have

told me this would have been me,

I would have laughed right at

you.

I woke up in the hospital.

No one was there, I never thought

hospitals were empty. Medicine

induced sleep cloaked the

atmosphere and settled into your

skin. Everything had that fake clean smell. Like a serial killer covering up his tracks- god I hate hospitals. I layed there after I discovered it was painful to move and that we probably shouldn't do that. It soon occurred to me that there was a feeding tube shoved up my nose, which was an experience. Fading in and out of consciousness like a flame that was about to go out, I slowly scanned my surroundings. I had the small room to myself and there was a tiny slit window in the corner. If I looked hard

enough I could see the sunrise
without having to move my neck.
The dull roar of a headache
persisted.

Continuing my search, my eyes
flickered over to a small piece
of paper on the bedside table.
Learning the art of moving my arm
slowly enough to reach for it, my
headache got a bit worse.
Grasping the fragile note in my
hand, I crained my neck to try
and make out the words.

woulda been here when

you woke up, but got some problems myself. I'm in room 4245, I'll visit when I can. Thank Kevin for me for bringing you here.

Everything,

Jack

Everything. That was what we said to each other. We didn't want to go through the hassle of good bye, the pressure of I love you, the danger of telling the other one to stay safe. So we say everything. My eyes poured over

the comforting words once more
and the burning questions
smouldered in the back of my
mind. Why was Jack in the
hospital too? I knew he wasn't in
the best of shape either but
exactly how bad off are we? What
did he mean thank Kevin for me?
He brought me here?

My head twinged in a brutal
protest to my ceaseless worrying.
I laid my head back on the pillow
and focused on my breathing.
Relaxing my muscles, I thought,
in and out, in and out. I closed

my eyes and once more fell into a fitful sleep.

A nurse hustled purposefully around the room, pulling me out of my slumber. She immediately bustled over to me as if me opening my eyes was a signal to worry over me. She clucked the typical questions, asking how I felt, what I remembered, could I move my toes, do you want water. I managed to try and smile at her but I must have looked like a failed picasso portrait. Her eyebrows wrinkled together as she adjusted the tube. I stared at

her innocently and she motioned

for the doctor.

He was the most stereotypical man

I've ever seen in my life. He

took long confident strides and

produced his

I'm-concerned-but-I-don't-make-mi

stakes-so-don't-worry look. A

precise balance between a

wrinkling eyebrow, crinkled eye,

and pursed lip. He mentions his

name but I don't catch it, I

decide to call him Dr. Doctor.

Wiping away an invisible drop of

sweat, he leans on the foot of the bed. Gesturing wildly, he calls me sweetheart about five times too many. "Lemme tell ya, sweetheart, you really gave those friends of yours a scare." Pulling out his clipboard, he begins down the line of 'concerns'.

Clearing his throat, he begins, "High traces of drugs. Bruising to the face, neck, chest, shoulders, back, abdomen, legs, and arms. Blood to alcohol

ratio was incredibly high. Cuts
and scrapes on above mentioned
areas. Severely malnourished and
underweight. Possible spine
damage. Kidney failure." He
pauses and stares at me,
searching for a reaction.

I mutter a question about my
kidneys. And an apology.

He goes on this long rant
about how all the drugs and
alcohol were messing with my
insides. He mumbled off something
about my stomach, liver, and

lungs, but I wasn't really listening. I stared out the window at the busy city. I watched people come of their apartments like animals do when they wake up from hibernation. Spring was coming. Everything looked a little brighter, the air felt a little warmer. I smiled to myself at the thought of the upcoming months.

Dr. Doctor snaps his fingers at me, angry that I wasn't responding correctly to the tragedy that had become my reality. His words come out sharper the before, "You have days before both of your kidneys shut down for good. Don't you understand? You're dying!" I stare at him blankly before muttering, "Dying would be an awfully great adventure."

Flustered, he throws his clipboard on my bed and tells me to either get a transplant and a better attitude or die. Looking down at the papers, I read in the top right corner, *apologize to*

Velma.

The nurse looks around
nervously. She resembles a deer
caught in the headlights of your
car...While it was munching away
at your flowers. I close my eyes
and sleep.

I wake up to hushed whispers
at my bedside. I keep my eyes
shut to try and eavesdrop.
Listening intently, I quickly
recognize the voices- Kevin and
Jack. They're in a silent war
with each other over my safety

and happiness. Jack's stance is
that I should stay here in
Chicago at the apartment so we
can take care of each other.
Kevin's is something resembling
locking me in a hospital in till
I'm 'me' again. I ponder whether
or not it's possible to ever stop
being yourself.

        Opening my eyes and
adjusting the wretched feeding
tube, they both stare at me
intently. At an attempt to

salvage any dignity I had left, I
tried to smile and asked how
their morning was going.

Kevin immediately starts
apologizing, his eyes flicking
back and forth over my wounds.
Those same eyes I saw the night
before fill with tears as if this
is the first time he's seen the
damage that he caused. Jack
watches the scene, completely
oblivious to how I got them.
Kevin probably said that I got
jumped or something to that
effect. He wasn't any good at

accepting the fact that he hurts
me. I ask Jack why he was staying
in the hospital. Caught off
guard, he sputters something
about drugs and weight and
whatever else and how
everything's better and that it's
important that I'm okay. I don't
ask him anymore questions because
I'm afraid I'll break him.

Kevin leans down and
whispers in my ear, apologizing
and telling me he loves me. His
breath is hot and he smells like
smoke and bad memories. He

suffocates me. Pleading that I was weak and felt funny, I asked if they could visit some other time. Jack looked like he was about to cry as he said to the floor that he had to work. Kevin immediately responded with a yes-anything-for-you-because-I-love-you. But it came out sounding like a question so I closed my eyes and hoped they would leave. Jack sniffled and left quietly. Kevin lingered long enough to kiss my hand. It burned. Again, I slept.

I woke up to a setting similar to the one when I first got here. It was late at night and everything had this eerie quiet to it. I'd been laying in this bed for the past day or so with little adventure outside of the confined room so I thought it'd be a good time to explore. Bracing myself, I slowly lifted myself up and out of the bed. Every muscle screamed in protest but I continued on. I banged my toe on the side of the bed and silently cursed the entire

facility. Pulling on a sweatshirt
and a second pair of fuzzy socks
from the bag the boys brought, I
made my way down the long
corridor.

The hallway was sterile and
chilly. All the doors were
closed, giving it a reject horror
movie sort of feel. It would have
been scarier if the lights
weren't so bright. Walking around
aimlessly, I eventually stumble
upon an official looking
elevator. Pulling the sleeves of
my sweatshirt over my hands, I

look up and study a bright and informative sign. The floors were organized by color! First floor was the lobby, red. Second, blue, was the children's area. Third was the terminal area, in grey. That was the floor I was on. Fourth was in yellow, that was just the floor for everyone else. And the fifth floor was green, that was the 'mental care unit'. Crazy people, thank God. I was beginning to think I was the only one.

The synchronized beeps of

the passing floors were a simple reminder of life outside the hospital. See, that was the thing, being in a hospital for an extended amount of time is like being in your own little society. I thought I should at least try and be social. So I went and tried my luck on the fifth floor. Seeing that it was past midnight, I wasn't sure what type of people I'd run into. And with that, the elevator doors slid open.

I carefully inch my way down the hallway, taking in my

surroundings. It resembles the rest of the floors except it's maybe a little greyer and there's a few of those motivational posters on the walls. I stop and stare at one that has a picture of a flower and reads, *it's okay to say you're not okay.* You know, if people were serious about helping the people in here, they wouldn't treat them like such a joke. I continue through the hall. About halfway down, I hear the faint sound of crying. Following the sound, I eventually stumble upon a scrawny looking boy of about 7. He's curled up in a ball and acting like he doesn't exist. The word 'sorry' is scribbled at least a hundred times on the wall next to him.

I sit down quietly next to him and gently put my arm around him. He immediately tenses up and stares at me. I apologize and ask if he's okay. He points at the flower poster. Smiling, I tell him I like him. Wiping his eyes, he looks over at me shyly and smiles back. He begins explaining that he missed his brother and

that he forgot to take his
medicine and no one brought it to
him. He informs me that no one
ever brings it and that he's
quite forgetful. About then,
another lanky guy walks over. His
eyes shift from the boy to me.
Registering that I'm not a
doctor, he immediately starts
apologizing. I stand up quickly
and apologize back. We're getting
nowhere.

I stick out my hand and
introduce myself. He smiles shyly

and mumbles to the floor, "Well, uh, I'm, uh, Kenny and uh, that's my brother Stephen and uh, you're you and uh."

I couldn't stop laughing. We both sit back down on the floor together. Firing off the questions, we all lean closer, immersed in the conversation. Hours must have passed by, because when I glance out the window I can see the sun beginning to rise. I felt more excited about life then I had in years. There was this strong sense of hope that just flowed between us.

I eventually found out that they're both patients here, his brother for schizophrenia and himself for attempted suicide. We both silently exchange glances at scarred wrists, he nods knowingly at me. For the first time, I didn't feel judged. It was this quiet acceptance, a muffled promise. He asks what's I'm 'in for'.

Beginning to ramble off the

whole story, I try not to gloss over the details about what actually happened. He stares at me intently, absorbing what I had to say. When I start slowing down, he reassures my doubts my touching my arm, like a little reminder that he wanted to know. I tell him about the books that I read, the people that I trust, I speak of Jack and the parties I had gone to. I tell him about modeling, how much I crave being someone else. I tell him about my Golden Tragedy. But I finally finish by saying, "And now I'm on the fifth floor of a hospital with my kidneys failing and if I don't get an immediate transplant, I die. Let me tell you, I don't give a damn at this point. Curtains got to close at some point, you know?"

He gets this sudden realization on his face and he mumbles, "You can't die."

Tilting my head, I ask why not.

He states matter of factly,

"I just so happen to have an extra kidney that I'm not using and it has your name on it." I look at him, completely perplexed. Getting my head around the fact that he was in the process of saving my life, still hasn't exactly happened.

He studies invisible things on the floor. His words poured out all at once, as if this is what he had always needed to say. The speed of his words was refreshing. Beginning, he sputters, "I'm convinced this is what had to happen. I'm in this place because I wanted to die, saving you would save me. You bring this complete light with you and I'm finally starting to figure out what tomorrow really is. It's so hard to explain because I've just met you, but I already trust you more then people I've known my whole life. Please, let me do this for you."

I sit, stunned. There are tears that burn and fill and spill. There are so many tears. We are all crying, we are all broken. But this unmistakable hope, it was so undeniable in that very moment. The papers would be signed in the next couple hours. We all sat there, holding each other. Stephen begins to hum, causing Kenny and I to laugh. That's the most beautiful sound, laughter after someone's been crying. It's raw and it demands to be cherished in the best of ways.

A nurse walked in, baffled at the scene. She reminds me of my nurse downstairs.

Grinning,Kenny stands up and announces, "Karen, I have the *privilege* of donating my kidney to this lovely lady and I need the paperwork to do so by tomorrow." Karen was confused. Kenny begins to explain the whole story and I throw in the name of my doctor. She says she'll 'see what she can do'. Hugging each other tightly, I depart back to my room. I strut down the lonely hallways, revived with the promise of a second chance.

A couple hours later,

Dr.Doctor comes into my room tentatively. Looking me up and down, he exclaims that this was an impossibility. That the transplant simply could not take place within the next twenty four hours. I ask him if he'd apologized to Velma. He pauses and struggles to find words. Staring at his shoes, he whispers, it will be done.

I'd like to tell you that it was this great process and that I was saved and we ran off into the sunset together. I woke up four

hours later and hurled
everything. Again and again and
again. I curled onto the cold
linoleum floor, trying to
disappear. Clawing at my
bandages, I couldn't stop
shaking. Remnants of a vivid
nightmare haunted me. I
remembered his grin, his touch,
his grip, and those eyes. The
eyes that would haunt me forever-
I was terrified. The various
machines I had been chained to,
squealed loudly in protest to my
breakdown. Dr. Doctor and my
nurse ran in promptly. My nose

was bleeding and I'd ripped the feeding tube out. Dr. Doctor stares at the nurse and tells her to get Kenny because it was time. Grabbing my arm, he shoved a sedative into my veins.

Kenny later told me he wasn't nervous for the surgery. I told him the monsters in my head had been screaming at me again. He laughed.

My insides hurt. Felt a little lighter I suppose, but maybe I was just fooling myself because I could finally sleep for a normal eight hours instead of 22 a day or not at all. That was a perk. I suppose another one was that I wasn't going to die. And when I say suppose, I really mean it's a miracle. I only had to stay for a couple of more days to get my strength back up, I was scheduled to leave the day after I got out.

The last night I was there, we all decided to meet where we first did. Looking out at the city lights, Kenny asked if I was scared. Staring out the window, it occurred to me that the lights look a lot like stars, they were twinkling. I smiled and shook my head, but I told him yes. No one knew that I got the surgery, I hadn't spoken to anyone. I figured I'd just walk back to the apartment and continue on like usual.

For a while, we just sat, staring. We were all lost in our own thoughts. Kenny was getting out in a couple days and Stephen in a week. There was never a more eloquent silence.

So I thanked him the best I could. How exactly does one thank someone for giving up on of their organs for you? This is a question I don't think I'll ever get the answer to. We promised we'd keep in touch and he made the joke that a part of him would always be with me. I laughed at that.

We stayed and sat together in till the sun rose. Kenny and I promised to see each other again.

Hugging him tightly, my nose stung with that about-to-cry sensation. When I looked up at him, he was already tearing up. We laughed at that.

Walking down that hallway, I felt that same feeling that you'd get when you'd leave summer camp. It completely sucked but you know you'll miss it. The fake hygiene of the place was starting to grow on me. There were so many people I hadn't met...

I stepped out of the

building with a fake confidence.
A feux ego. I felt as if I didn't
belong to the city anymore,
everything seemed so foreign. The
sky high buildings suddenly
didn't seem so high, people
looked busy and uninterested.
I'll blame it on the fact that I
was sober.

I sauntered down the
familiar streets, tracing my way
back to our little apartment.
Climbing up the stairs, nerves
fluttered around my stomach. It
seemed so silly to be afraid to

walk into the apartment. I forced
myself to open the door.

He is hunched over. He is
shaking. He does not look up at
me. He is crying. He has
bloodshot eyes. He is starving, I
can count his bones. He is dying.

My first thought was to run.
Was to run away from everything
bad in my life. But it occurred
to me that it would catch up to
me, it always does. So I decide
to walk. I walk over to him and I
hug him. I hug him like that's

what will fix him, hug him like I
can fix everything.

He does not speak to me, I
wonder if he has lost his words.
Holding his head, he looks at me
with broken eyes. And with that,
I understand.

It is silly how people
depend on words so much, they
lose the connection, the strength
of silence. I know, I understand.

I kiss his forehead and tell
him I'm going to get soup and

muffins. He smiles with those eyes.

I know of a little shop that sells soup and muffins. It's just down the block. The sun warms my face, as if it was trying to tell me it was going to be okay. The shop was just down the block. But he was there, watching, smiling. His smile did not meet his eyes. Kevin tries to catch up to me but I run. Running away from him, I feel like I am 8 years old again, that I can outrun everyone and everything. I pretend I am lightning.

I duck into the shop but he finds
me. He grabs my wrist and pulls
me back. I fall into him and his
arms envelope me, enclosing me
into his body like a Christmas
present that nobody wants.

Nuzzling into my neck, his
breath is hot and ragged. "I've
missed you," he exhales, "I don't
know how I'll ever live without
you. Please, baby, forgive me. I
never meant to hurt you." My head
pleaded no, my heart announced

yes. My body tensed, but my words came out like honey. Sticky sweet, I smiled and told him I missed him. He kisses my cheek and tells me it's great to see me well again and that he was worried sick. I don't tell him about my kidney. I don't tell him about how he's shattering every inch of progress I had made. I don't tell him that his very claws are what's dragging me to my own personal hell. I smile like a good girl. Because that's what he wants. Because that's what he needs. Because I love him.

We buy the food and drop it
off at the apartment but we don't
stay. He takes my hand and leads
me back. Back as if he could turn
back time and take away all the
little flaws and tarnishes that
have dented our relationship. All
the little pick-me sized cuts
that he carved into my heart. So
with words like an eraser, he
leads me into that little
bookshop where we first met. He
sits me down in that little booth
and whispers love poems and

apologies. He describes a better future for the both of us like a real estate agent would flaunt a piece of property and I give in. I accept. I believe. He convinces me to come back in June. He controls me like a puppet, manipulating every smile, every word. He moves my fingers to the buttons on his phone, causing them to type the very numbers that would lead him to my voice, every time.

The sun is setting and we walk down a forgotten trail in a

forgotten park. It is so odd, that trail. You look beyond the trees and see the skyscrapers. I think about how my life is like this. The trees are home, the skyscrapers are here. Meshed together in the messiest of ways, I am the litter at the gateway. Forgotten and unwanted. He kisses my nose and tells me I'm adorable. He is so pleased with himself. I am *happy*.

   My facade is unparalleled. I am an actress in my own life. I chose my words like a writer

would create the script. I smile
and giggle and blush. I am so
good at this.

He peers into my eyes and I
wonder if he can read the lies
behind them. If he can, he does
not say. He clings to me.
Whispering that he loves me.

I tell him to not make such
a mistake. He laughs at that.

We walk, our bodies
connecting each other like pieces
in a puzzle. Strangers smile at

the picture of young love. So why is it that I feel so old? Why is it, that I feel I have walk a thousand miles? Lived a hundred lives? Why could I tell you my name, but not describe the person it is connected with? I lie to myself.

Just for tonight, I will lie. I will lie and he will believe. It is for him, everything is for him.

This toxic love is what poisons me. It rots my heart.

He kisses me good night. He
tells me he loves me again. He
gets tears in his eyes, I make
mine do the same. We promise to
keep in touch, I promise to
return.

I make my way up the stairs,
head down, defeated. Opening the
door, Jack nods knowingly. He
extends a handful of pills and I
swallow them all at once. I begin
to fade, to forget. My vision
blurs, my hands shake, the voices
in my head quiet. I am peaceful,

I am enchanted, falsely
enlightened.

This plastic happiness will
have to do. We float out the
window together, light like snow,
pure like rain. We howl and yelp
at the city below, clinging to
the fire escape because it felt
like we could float away. We were
drowning in our self loathing, in
our sin. Yet we could fly.

We press our palms together,
vowing to stay safe, to hide from
the demons. We look into each

other's eyes and understand. He see's me and I see him. It is simple, it is all so simple. I lie my head on his lap and look up. I pretend that is chin is part of the sky, his eyes, stars. "It is a beautiful hell," he tells me, "I apologize for bringing you down with me, angel." I laugh and tell him it was okay. Everything was a-okay. We absorb the unsaid words and feast on weeks memories. The sun rises like an hourglass in reverse. I was going to return home soon. A feeling, impossible

to describe, settles in my
stomach and will stay dormant in
till I walk through that same
apartment door once more. I am
scared for the upcoming months.

Jack tells me he'll miss me
before I go. Tells me he'll be
right where I left him. He
reminds me of an old toy, a teddy
bear with a missing eye perhaps.
Chewing my lip, he laughs at me.
He tells me I think too much. I
tell him he thinks too little. He
shakes his head and laughs,
telling me his mission is to get

his thoughts to cease.

I board the plane I rise
above it all.

Part Two

I stand before the mirror
once more, eyes like daggers. The

one looking back is mean, but I am meaner. I mutter, I spit, I insult. But everything I say is just a fancy spin off of a simple statement: You are fat. I close my eyes, remembering my mother's simple words. "Have you gained weight?" Tears burn my cheeks like fire and I look at the girl in the mirror once again, contemplating what she would look like with all the burn scars. You know, sometimes I wonder what would happen if the pain we feel inside was reflected like a bruise, a scrape. Would I ever heal? Or am I simply doomed to the picking of a scab not keen on being forgotten?

The black lines of my watery makeup traces my checks, flowing down like little rivers. I recall the words of a movie I once saw, a girl looking in the mirror and her friend asking her, "What do you see?"

I see scabbed lips and too many nights of shoving words unsaid down my own throat. I see protruding collar bones, a sharp reminder of what I can and can not have. I see prominent ribs, gashes across the flesh of my shrinking stomach. I restrict, I restrain, I control. I see hip bones, jutting out like a cry for help. Paper skin, stretched over my dying frame.

I deem the mirror a liar. I am fat, I am flubber, I am lard. I disgust myself. I pray to a God that I doubt, that I've never been sure of believing in. But I whisper, I plead, make me skin and bones. Let me disappear. Make me sane.

Mirror, mirror, suiting you has become my purpose. You are oh so ruthless to your victims. Hunger persisting, will fading, I am worthless. I must be skinny.

Mirror, mirror, can't you see? The things you show are slowly killing me.

Skinny, is my monsters whisper.

Skinny, is what my thoughts spit.

I shall hide in my baggy clothing, so no one will know that I have been defeated.

The idea of starving myself until I disappear is enticing. The thought of swallowing pills that falsely take the pain away is tempting. The image of drowning in a bathtub is beautiful.

I decide that I need help.

So I call Kenny. He answers on the first ring. "What's up

buttercup?"

"I'm thirty four pounds underweight, I'm swallowing pills like it's my damn job, I'm in an abusive relationship, and my feet are cold."

He laughs sadly, I could almost see him shaking his head as he responds, "Darling put some socks on. Find the deepest shade of red lipstick to ever exist, strike the fear of God into a man's heart, and get some help."

I sigh and bend down to scope out my lipstick colors, "Oh I know it. Maybe if I state it frankly my mom will figure out that she needs to pay some hospital bills. Thought I was done with all of this."

"It never ends."

So with wringing hands and a heavy heart, I make my way downstairs. My mother peers at me over a glass of red wine. I pounder getting her a bucket so she wouldn't have to make so many god damn trips to the fridge. Her mouth curls and she leans forward, taking satisfaction in my confessions. Maybe I should get a white flag and set it on fire for added effect? I am no good at talking, I am no good at asking for help. I'm too much of a coward to admit when I am in need.

So she watches me with red, wine soaked lips. If she was a cartoon, she would be made of mouth.

*Stop speaking, don't you see
what I'm trying to say, stop
speaking, please let me tell you,
stop speaking, stop interrupting,
no you did not know it all a
long, SHUT UP.*

And so it clicks. She tilts
her head and musters tears,
sniffling obnoxiously. Searching
for sympathy like a dog would for
a bone. I am calling her a dog
because I already cursed once on
this page.

She nods and clucks about

checking me into a 'helpful center' by noon tomorrow. Is this was progress feels like? Am I supposed to be feeling proud for 'taking a step in the right direction'? Should I be happy yet? I am not proud, I am not happy. I retreat to my bedroom and pack my bags.

She drops me off and tells me to 'get better'. I mull over if a mental illness is something where you can take your pills and be cured.

Walking in, I spot a disheveled looking women manning the front desk. I give her the general information, weight, height, sex, reason for staying, date of birth. When we finish, she looks up at me through crooked glasses and tells me that we don't mess around and that I must be committed to getting through my disorder. I make silent observations regarding her dark circles.

You know, I never liked the word disorder. It sounds like a

mess, a disarray, a problem. Just because I picked up the habit of eating exactly 200 calories a day and I can recite to you the nutrition facts of 64 popular foods does not mean that I am broken. Just because I sometimes can not manage to get out of bed in the morning because *there is literally no point*, does not mean that I am broken. Just because my depression is caused by a chemical imbalance in my brain and that most people can not seem to understand that no, I actually don't want attention, does not

mean that I am broken. Just
because I depend on my sadness to
act as old paint under new and
that I am forced to wear my
anxiety like hand-me-down jeans,
does not mean that I am broken.
Just because when a news reporter
claims that a meteor might hit
Earth,that I am not worrying that
it will hit me, but that it will
hit a nuclear power plant, does
not mean that I am broken. If all
of this was a 'disorder' in my
head, then I would have cleaned
the mess myself.

The girls stare at me behind
thinning hair and dead eyes. The
lady sits me down and takes my
bag and I get a minor flashback
to the fifth grade. The girls
didn't like me there either. She
introduces me as if I was a fun
fact, flaunting the obvious
statement that I'm 'new here', as
if no one could tell. She is
shooed away with glares and
stares, uninterested sighs and
yawns. We didn't come to make
friends. I open my book and read.

After a little while, a

slender lady touches my shoulder and asks me what I'm reading. I tell her, "Gatsby." She laughs gently, a pathetic attempt at hiding the fact she's never heard of it. The audacity. She then smiles wider, asking me if I want to come and 'chat'. Quickly deciding that I want to yank that smile off of her face, I tell her no. Apparently, I didn't really have a choice. I fantasize about breaking her teeth as if they were a fancy glass vase.

So she leads me through a

few dimly lit hallways into a little grey room. The color of the wall matches the color of her hair, but I think my hair would be grey to if I had to work in a building that smelled and looked like death. I see a picture of a little girl playing in the sand on a beach. It is the only thing colorful in the room.

She sits cross legged in her chair, just like me. I quickly regurgitate a fact about how people mimic who they're talking to so they seem more trustworthy.

I then tell her she can put her legs down. She forces a smile and asks what is wrong. I stare at her.

"Frankly, that is a stupid question. Let's not talk emotions and feelings, let's not dance around the subject. I don't want to be here and you're secretly sitting there thinking that you aren't being paid enough to do this."

She sputters that she is only here to help me. She talks

firmly, trying to remind me who's the boss here. She tells me we need to deal with the real problems. Arming herself with a pen and a pad of paper, she asks again, what is wrong.

I stare her dead in the eyes and say it. I say it like I'm not shaking, like I'm not crying, like I am not scared. "I'm all strung out on drugs and pain, princess. I've been touched and hit and abused. Locked bedroom doors make me anxious and that is not a metaphor. Honestly, you couldn't help me if you tried. Look at me. You know what's wrong."

She sits there, furiously scribbling on her paper. Glancing up at me, she spits, "Don't act like you don't need help. You're dying and you know it. You have no control anymore. I'm the last chance you've got. Your trauma could have been stopped, you shouldn't have gotten involved with him in the first place."

I've never been more angry

in my life. I was speaking to the floor, but I decided it was time to stand up for myself. "You know what? I sold every inch of my body and called it art. And when you sit here and call rape something else, you sound a lot like him. Except he didn't call it a trauma, he called it love."

And I suppose that's the story of how I did a complete 180 and got kicked out of rehab.

I *strutted* to that little

dorm and I grabbed my bags. I
marched past those stupid girls.
They stared at me as if they were
behind bars and I had just found
the means of escape. Applying my
lipstick, I asked the
receptionist if I could use the
phone. She told me no. So I took
it.

Punching in the numbers of
my house, I stared at her
defiantly. My mom readily agreed
to pick me up. It would be bad
for our reputation if anyone saw
me here. For once in my life, I

was feeling empowered. I leaned against the wall and smoked a cigarette right then and there. I could feel the eyes on me, the hate of a starved addiction crowding the air more than the smoke coming from my cigar.

I saw the familiar car pull up at the entrance. Hooking the cigarette between my teeth, I reached for my bags and marched my skinny ass out of there. I quickly started to question myself, the words of the grey lady haunting me. I watched the stars as we drove home, hoping to find an answer.

I'd like to tell you the upcoming weeks were better, and in some ways they were. But the truth of it was that I never got the help that I needed and I was in the end going to regret walking out those doors, just like I thought I would.

Kevin ended up calling me the night I got back. Funny how these things have a way of occurring. It was 2 AM and I was alone. I answered. He asked me how I was. That's thing about those words, they make you feel loved so you trust and you give. *How are you.* Damn.

I would have let him pull open my ribs and pluck them like cello strings if that's what he was into. I was starving for someone who cared and he was ready to suffocate me. When we love, we love deeply, and for so long. So there I was, laying flat on my back, phone pressed to my check, smiling through the tears.

I could feel myself forgiving
him, feel myself slipping into
his words like they were gorgeous
white gloves; it was all so
beautiful to me. He said sorry
and his voice was like glass. He
said I love you and that glass
was suddenly stained and
beautiful. You could see the sun
shining through it with every
promise he made. Tell me, is it
beautiful tragic or tragically
beautiful?

"Angel," He whispers, "Pull
your blankets up. I don't want

you to be cold, especially if I can't be there to hold you in my arms." I smile and settle down in the blankets. Everything was so cozy and inviting, the fabric to his voice to the stars in the sky. Through the comforting haze of sleep, I tell him I love him. He says it back.

Isn't that the greatest thing? When they say it back? You and your lover are in that in between state of being awake and tumbling into sleep. Wanting to whisper to each other, but

wanting to indulge on the silence
all at the same time. So you do a
little bit of both and it's just
perfect. Everything is so right.

With a hint in insecurity,
he tentatively asks, "What do you
think of me?"

I sigh and stare up at my
ceiling, as if the textured white
surface would somehow spell out
the words I was so desperately
searching for. You know, I really
hate when people ask these types
of questions. It's almost as bad

as someone saying, *describe yourself.*

Taking a deep breath, I begin, "You know, I never meant to fall in love with you. I should hate you, I should stay as far away from you as I possibly can. I should be cursing your very being if I was smart. But we're here and we're talking and everything feels so right for once. I'm not paranoid about that noise outside, I'm not wondering if I locked my door. For once in my life, all the incessant noise

in my head has silenced. I wasn't
supposed to need you like this,
but you smiled and I blew it."

He didn't say anything at
first. But I could feel him
smiling, I could feel his
contentment in my bones. It was
the same thing I was feeling. But
I was the one that made him
happy. This, this is good. He
breathes out, as if he was trying
to exhale his happiness and share
it with me. Like giving me his
smile for the gift of my words.
"I love you," He sighs, "But I

worry about you. It is so sad, you are so strong and lovely, I forget that you are struggling."

I shudder at the word. The cold that I had thought I was protected from returns, rattling my fragile frame. "That's my problem," I begin unsteadily, "I define my absolute value from zero. If I'm a size one, then I'm one size away, so I'm fat. If I'm a size zero, then I'll want them to make a negative one just so I can starve myself to get there. It's an endless struggle. These thoughts..You don't understand..They prick at your heart and pull at your soul, they take over your mind and drag you down. Why is it that everyone tells me I'm beautiful but it feels like the world's best kept secret? I want to keep smashing myself until I am whole.." My voice drags off, my thoughts are consuming me. I think of dozens of judging eyes, roaming up and down my body without permission. Swallowing, consuming every ounce of dignity I could ever hope to have.

"Don't cry, please don't cry. I need you to listen to me-you deserve to live. You deserve to thrive and flower and bloom. Tell me, when your loved ones carry your coffin, do you want them to doubt that there's a body in there? That's the road you're headed down." He speaks firmly, as if I was an unruly child and this was his last idea for discipline. It as if he is begging me to hear his words.

Staring into a mirror on the

wall, I can faintly see the outline of my body through the darkness. Mumbling more to myself than anyone else, I whisper, "I see humans but no humanity." I hang up the phone without telling him good night.

So I lie awake, shivering from the cold, sweating from my nerves. It is nights like these where I question everything. I want to scream, yet my lips will not part. Folding myself into the depths of my bed, I drift into a fitful slumber.

I am standing on a pier,
mist surrounds me and it glides
across the smooth water. It is
all so quiet. I stare into the
crystal clear water, watching my
reflection. I see a girl behind
me in the reflection. I do not
turn to check. She is whispering
her secrets in my ear. I watch
her grab me and slowly twist my
bones, bending my frame to fit
the mold she has forced upon me.
I am skinny.

I wake up the next morning

with little red marks all over my body. My nails are bloody, my jaw is clenched so tightly that I have a headache. Examining the damage in the mirror, I begin to connect the dots. I had dug my nails into my skin while I was asleep. As if I didn't have enough problems, now it looks like I wrestled with a potato peeler. Throwing on a baggy sweatshirt, I make my way downstairs in desperate search for liquid, caffeinated encouragement. No one was home so I curled up on the couch and listened to Tyra Banks rant and rave about how I was 'so worth it'. I chuckle at her. Tyra, what about the skinny girls that aren't pretty enough to be models on your fancy runway? I'd rather be anorexic and posing in Europe then anorexic and posing in basement studios. Just saying.

Staring out the window, I watch brave bumblebees swarm around the new flowers. Pulling on some boots, I venture outside. Following my memory, I eventually trace my way to the place where

Jack first took me. I explore the trails and eventually stumble upon the lake.

Looking across the water, I suck in my cheeks. It was so odd being back here, when it had been almost six months. Sitting down on the bank, I took in every detail. The trees that lined the body of water looked like a bunch of adolescents. Tall and spindly, still growing into their new leaves. Dead branches stuck at the top seem to be reaching up to heaven.

Getting my fill of the landscape, I make my way back home. It was always the strangest thing, going back. Stepping off the trail was like flipping the light on in the middle of the night. The suburban area just feels so overpowering, like the light would. But closing my eyes doesn't help.

I suppose you could say I was depressed. I was eating again, sort of. Except every bite was a battle, the subject of my sanity, a war. Little red cuts

line my body, like markers for
soldiers lost. There are larger
gashes, but those are mostly on
my wrists. I don't have a
metaphor for those yet.

My safe haven was the
shower. See, you can't mess up
taking a shower. Yeah, you could
argue that you might get shampoo
in your eyes, but that happens to
everyone. No matter what you do,
theres always one simple,
attainable goal: get clean.
Nothing could go wrong. But I've
been experimenting with water

temperature to figure out what makes a 'perfect' shower and I was also trying to find a metaphor for the cuts on my wrists. I realized that the whole thing is a lot like taking a hot shower.

See, you get in and it hurts a bit because of the temperature. But you get used to it and stay because it's warm. You even begin to enjoy it- lots of people take hot showers after they've had a stressful day. It calms you down. Except, your skin is all red when you step out. No one ever talks about that part. That is where I found the metaphor.

Essentially, that helped nothing. But I felt like I was a step closer. Watching the days tick by, it was almost June. May was one of those weird months. You're happy that it exists but you sort of want it to end. It's like a little kid playing violin-it's adorable, but they don't know what they're doing yet.

So the days until Chicago

dwindled like the number on the
scale. The amount of scars on my
body increased, as did the amount
of nights Kevin and I fell asleep
on the phone together. It was
almost nice belonging to somebody
like that. If everything else was
a complete mess, I could at least
count on his voice coming through
the static. He was my anchor.

On a particularly warm
night, I stared at the stars as
he told me little details of his
day. That's what I loved most-
just listening to him. He was

this amazing storyteller, he knew exactly which words to string together to orchestrate something as simple as how his day went. Sometimes, it would get so detailed that I could easily close my eyes and imagine that I went through it all with him.

"Angel," He mumbled lazily. I grinned at his sleepy voice. "I can hear your smile but my eyes are craving you. Tell me you'll be here soon."

"Just close your eyes.

You're so tired. I'm right next to you- but don't try to touch me. I'm just out of reach, but I'm right there." I pulled the blanket up to my chin, even though it was at least 80 outside. I was always so cold.

We laid in silence, smiling at each other through the phone. This distance, it kills. But you learn to appreciate the little things. I learned his voice with the same amount of detail that I used on memorizing his hands. I got the courage to tell him about that one night. He laughed and called me cute. I had never been called cute before. Not thinking, I remember asking him, "What is a cute?" He laughed really hard at that. I tried to disappear.

This would be the last night that we'd have to depend on the static representation of the other one's voice. I was going to see him in less than 24 hours time. I would tell you something girly, like I had butterflies about seeing him again, but I'd be lying. It was more like those cockroaches that could survive the zombie apocalypse. That's what was in my stomach.

Saying good-bye to my mother was always a precarious situation. I didn't want to disappoint her by not being affectionate enough, but I didn't want to have the expectation of her actually missing me. So we did this awkward half hug. Like two extremely homophobic men hugging each other. It was a glorified pat on the back, essentially. Except we didn't end

it by yelling, "No homo!" We
weren't that bad.

Planes were always nice
though. They were so futuristic
to me, but I guess you could call
me archaic for that. The flight
attendant's plastic friendliness
is comforting in a twisted way. I
know she's being paid to ask how
my day is, but it's nice to
pretend she really cares. And
then she gives you little
pretzels and it's just so
adorable. It's like a separate
world up there, honestly. Being a

pilot is one of those jobs I know I'll never actually go for, but wouldn't mind having. The clouds are so gorgeous and everything is so quiet and protected. Sometimes, you can see the sunrise or the sunset. And don't even get me started about flying at night. Ugh, perfection.

I wouldn't mind just spending my whole life on one giant plane ride. I don't care about where I'm coming from or where I'm going. I just want to feel safe and eat free pretzels.

Maybe instead of sending people
to jail, we could send them on
plane rides so they can have some
time to wind down and reflect on
things. I think that'd be better.
It's like one of those wilderness
programs, except no one dies.

We had a lot of unexpected
turbulence towards the end of the
flight. The voice over the
intercom tells people to put
their seatbelts on. I never took
mine off. The lady next to me
starts praying. I see a man in
front of me taking pills so he
won't look afraid. The plane

lurches, a couple others yell. I hear a little girl ask her mom, "Are we going to crash?" My first thought was 'oh well'.

And that scares me more then the plane crashing. Scares me more then everything catching on fire. Scares me more than sinking to the bottom of the ocean.

But we don't crash, we land safely. So the lady stops praying and the man in front of me doesn't look so scared. He calls his wife and tells her he loves

her. I get off the plane alone
and try to find Jack.

He smiles when I first see
him. It wasn't one of those
I'm-happy-to-see-you smiles, it
was a full out goofy grin. It is
my favorite thing that he does.
It's like when someone is talking
about something they're
passionate about and they get
those lights in their eyes. If
that was translated to a smile-
this would be it. Hugging me, he
picks me up and spins me around.
"I've missed you dear one!" He

gushes. My cheeks hurt from smiling so much. It's crazy, you never notice how much someone's absence affected you in till you see them again. Yeah, you miss them, but you don't really feel it in till they are standing right beside you.

He launches into telling me the latest drama, gesturing wildly for every new tidbit of information. The latest and greatest scandal is that Derek, my photographer and Jack's boss's girlfriend cheated on him. Not

once, but four times- in a week!
Jack quickly informs me that
we'll most likely be doing darker
shoots for the following weeks. I
don't object. There are plenty of
memories I can use for
inspiration to express the mood
of the photo. We walk briskly
down the crowded streets, each of
us with a bag in hand. He talks
as fast as he walks and I
struggle to keep up with what
he's telling me. Turning sharply
into the dank apartment building,
he reaches out and takes my bag.
"I'll be right back!" He calls

over his shoulder as he runs up the stairs, taking two at a time. "Don't move!"

I smile to myself. He's too adorable. I'd never really taken in the details of the lobby before. At first glance, it resembles one of those dime-a-dozen motel lobbies. But if you continue to search, you find all these lovely little aspects. I see a baby blue vase with pastel pink roses, perky and lively. An antique looking mirror hangs above a quirky table. I see a grey, almost metallic looking

chair in the corner. Adjacent

from it, a couch with a vintage

feel. The pieces brighten up the

grey-brown vibe the entire

building gives off. It's just all

so homey to me.

Jack returns, asking what

I'm smiling about. Shaking my

head, I tell him nothing. He

takes my hand and leads me out

into the sunshine. He walks

quickly, but doesn't tell me

where we're going when I ask.

"It's a surprise!" He calls over

his shoulder. I love seeing him so giddy. Suddenly, we duck into a little shop. Turning towards a flight of stairs tucked away in a corner, he gestures that we're going up. I look at him warily, but my curiosity gets the best of me; I follow eagerly.

Going up those stairs was almost like a scene out of one of those Narnia movies. With the wardrobe? That's the one. Reaching the top was like stepping into another world. The bottom floor was damp, like a reject Wal Mart. But the upper floor was covered head to toe in fabric. Peering around, I took in the merchandise. Glitter, satin, silk, sparkle, velvet, leather. It was adorable. A quirky looking women sits in the center, hunched over a sturdy looking sewing machine. It was bright yellow and the little needle worked as fast as lightning. She narrowed eyes behind bright purple, horned glasses. Obviously unhappy with a particular stitch. Solving the problem with some quick finger working, she sets in once again on the garment.

"Dahlia..?" Jack asks hesitantly. Her head immediately snaps up and she smiles. Standing up and adjusting her extravagant shawl, she extends her hand towards me. Shaking it, I glance down at the dozens of rings. One finger housed five, sparkling beauties. The next, three rubber ones. Catching my wondering eyes, she tilts her head and exclaims, "Aren't these just precious? I found 'em at an old diner last week. What a find!" All I could do was smile like an idiot and nod. "Oh you're such a gem!" She coos, "Absolutely adorable. I know just what I want to put you in." Jack stands back, proudly crossing his arms. She rushes into a back room, leaving only the scent of her overpowering, lilac perfume.

"Jack, tell me something," I begin, "What *exactly* are we doing here?" Looking around, I began to wonder about the price of these fabulous pieces. Nothing we could afford.

Sighing dramatically he starts, "Let me explain, darling. Derek said he needed something new for the shoots and parties when he heard you were coming back. So he told me to bring you here- and here we are!"

"Jack," I whisper, "We can't afford any of this!" He laughs and shakes his head, telling me not to worry. Apparently, it's all dirt cheap. This is her 'warehouse' and Derek's an old friend. Fine.

Just then, she waltzes in, arms heavy with clothing. Tossing the articles at me, she squeals with excitement. She points me to the direction of the dressing room and instructs me to try on *everything*. Locking myself in the closet space, I examine the clothing. There were four dresses, three pairs of pants, six tops, two pairs of shoes, and an insane amount of jewelry. Everything was black. Slipping into the first dress, I turn and look myself over in the mirror.

It was gorgeous. It was short,
shiny, and sassy. Strapping on
one pair of the heels, I opened
the door. She immediately gasps
dramatically and rushes over.
Touching and pulling and
adjusting, she steps back to
examine everything. Grinning, she
mumbles, "Ravishing darling,
simply devine."

Blushing, I retreat to the
dressing room to try on more
clothes. Hanging the dress back
on the hanger, I slowly make my
way through the stack of

clothing, showing each one off.
Once we're finally finished, she
waves us off, telling us to visit
soon. Jack smiles at me wildly as
we leave. I inform him that we
didn't pay. "Already covered." He
replies confidently. A giddy
excitement swells inside me. We
strut the rest of the way back to
the apartment.

Once we return, we realize
that it's just about sundown.
Jack proudly announces that we're
'going out'. I don't object and
retreat to the bathroom to begin

the ritual. I apply a new face.
Plucking at eyebrows, lengthening
eyelashes, I paint my lips a
seductive red. Looking in the
mirror, I almost don't recognize
who is looking back at me. I am a
representation of the city,
glossy, unattainable, and just a
bit dangerous. Strapping on my
heels, I see Jack smiling at me
out of the corner of my eye.
"It's so great to have you back."
He blushes and takes my arm.

"Glad to be back, darling."
I reply. My words are as warm as

the air outside. "You look
ravishing, by the way. Like a
true gentleman." It was true
though. Chic and slick, black
clothing in contrast with his icy
complexion. His height only added
to his confident stance. His eyes
reminded me of the city lights.
Dazzling and bright, enticing
you. We took a cab and rode on to
the gates of our sinful escape.

See, the club's nickname was
literally 'Hell'. No one even
knows the official name of the
club, or of the man who keeps it

up. The owner himself resembles
the Devil. He has a muscular
build, rough features, and dark,
unforgiving eyes. He sits in the
corner booth, perched on the
black leather. Every aspect of
his posture screams, 'danger,
stay away'. Drink on the table,
but never once have I seen him
take a sip. He watches
peacefully, eyes grazing over
each and every face, memorizing
their features. Countless girls
approach him, desperate to entice
him with hips, lips; countless
temptations inches away from his

face. But he does not crack, he
nods politely and stares on,
searching.

Rumor has it, he was once
horribly in love with a lady by
the name of Eve. Apparently her
hair was as red as her lips,
which were as red as the fire she
set to his heart. She used to
come every night, dancing in the
exact middle. He would openly
stare at her. She was the only
one he stood up for. When she got
tired, she would go over to the
booth and sleep on him. He would

watch her, mesmerized, tracing her features with careful hands. It was as if they were a life sized snowglobe, that the world really was just composed of him and her.

There is a mysterious black staircase tucked into the corner of the room, right near his booth. You'd never find it unless you were specifically looking for it. Apparently, one night he led her up those stairs. Some say he came back down alone, hours later. Others say he never came back at all, but simply reappeared at that same booth, watching as he does to this day. No one has seen Eve since, no one knows for sure what happened to her. Did he confess his love and find that the feeling was not mutual? Did she escape into the night, or was she killed?

I shudder whenever his eyes meet mine. It is a type of fear that grasps your innermost thoughts and pulls. It plays with your logic and dictates your pulse. Tell me, is my heart racing or did it completely stop? There is only one fear that does this- the fear of the unknown.

Avoiding his stare, I focus my attention on the bodies around me. The beat of the sound makes my head pound, crowding out my thoughts. Reaching for some pills in an outstretched hand, I wait for my worried thoughts to be crowded out. A peace washes over me, I feel as if I could dance forever. Sweaty bodies, eager palms, flashing lights, I look into people's eyes. Finding the

exact same thing in every pair, I
wonder, how is it that eyes can
be so bright, yet so dead, at the
same time?

As the night goes on, my
thoughts and vision becomes more
and more fuzzy. I am losing my
logic as if it is water in a
glass and I can't manage to stop
spilling it. I am tired, so
tired. We all are; yet we beat
ourselves ceaselessly into the
folds of the night, persistently
throwing every ounce of our
beings towards dawn. The feeling

was contagious, but it wasn't
something you could catch like a
cold. No- you infected yourself.
I locked myself up, I was the one
who swallowed the key. With gun
to temple, we annihilate
ourselves with a smile on our
face.

*Maybe if I dance enough,
I'll forget about what my sleeves
are hiding.*

*Maybe if I dance enough, I
won't think about what happened
the last time I was here.*

Maybe if I dance enough, I

*won't recall the fact that I
threw myself down the stairs the
other day, hoping I'd shatter
like glass.*

*Maybe if I dance enough,
I'll become someone else.*

I feel hands grabbing at me,
a tall man whispers in my ear. I
can feel his spit. "Aren't you a
pretty one?" He growls, "You can
be mine tonight." His grip
tightens. *No, no, no, no.* I
tactfully put bodies between his

and mine. I am shaking.

Coming here, I suppose I was hoping for a bit of a serendipity, except I was looking too hard, so it never came. All I saw were some serious looking men; very busy looking serious. I thought to myself, these are not men. These are just tall children, holding beers and conversations that they don't understand. I wanted to go home. But tell me, is home a place or a feeling? Because I don't feel much anymore.

Finding Jack, I realize that he's wasted, but not much happier than I. He searches my face, looking into my eyes. Tilting his head, he asks, "What's wrong, flower?"

I sigh and look at the ground. "You won't understand and I can't explain it." Looking up again I mumble, "Take me home?" Grinning at the idea of a job he could complete, he extends his arm and we walk out together. Jack rambles on and on about the stars, even though you can not see them, for it is raining. I smile at the simplicity of making him happy. If I could wish on one of these stars he's talking about, I would wish to be not so complex. I'm too busy trying to figure out happiness to be happy myself. I once heard a metaphor about happiness, something with a butterfly. It was something like, if you go chasing after it, you'll never catch it. But if you sit there quietly, it will simply land on your shoulder.

I don't know about you, but
I've sat outside quietly numerous
times, and butterflies don't land
on my shoulder.

As we approached the
building, a very familiar
silhouette leaned against the
brick. I felt myself smiling, yet
I didn't feel very happy. I had a
case of fleeting nerves, my
senses told me to run. And yet I
had somehow ended up in his arms.
"Kevin, great to see you!" Jack
beamed, shaking his hand.

"I could say the same to you, old sport." He replied smoothly. He winked at me as I grinned at the reference he made. He knew *The Great Gatsby* was my favorite. We had spent the past few weeks reading chapters to each other. Pulling me closer to him, he leaned down and kissed the top of my head. Inhaling deeply, he purrs, "I've missed you, angel."

I feel my cheeks getting hot. Stuttering and failing to reply, I nod. He laughs at that.

Taking my hand, he suggests we go
on a walk. I had no idea what
hour it was, but I was sure it
was something absurd. I agree and
walk with him.

We trace our way down to a
little forgotten park, we'd sort
of claimed it as our own. The
moon and the stars were the only
lights if you got far enough into
the trees. Giggling, we whispered
poetry to each other about
galaxies in our bones and moons
in our hearts. He sneezes and
makes a bad pun about stardust.

Adorable. I giggle and kiss his nose to show my gratitude of his...cuteness.

It was always so refreshing to be near him. He was so gentle with everything. His quietness was calming, his words like waves and I wanted to drown.

He turns towards me, his tall frame looming over me. Cupping my face, he studies my eyes and brushes a hair off my forehead. Leaning forward he whispers, "I see you in colours that don't exist."

Inhaling, he looks down at the ground, eyes too shy to meet mine. He stands quietly, holding my hands. He rubs his thumb over the ridges of my knuckles. Don't you love that? When someone does that?

"I love you with a passion that should not exist. I need you with an urgency that passes any form of logic. I miss you with a severity that has no business being real."

It was so much like one of those moments, where you're going upstairs and you think there's another step. You feel as if you're falling for a second, it's so unnerving because you were just climbing stairs and now it's like you're falling to your death. Theres truth but no logic. That's how his words to me felt, how they sounded, what they meant.

It was my turn to be too shy to look him in the eye. Worried,

he immediately asks what's wrong.
Shaking my head, I tell him I'm
just tired. Draping his jacket
over my shoulders, he leads me
back towards the city. He feels
dejected and I'm feeling guilty.

But honestly, how could I
respond? My brain's screaming at
me, telling me to run as fast and
as far as I can. But my heart is
persuading me that his arms are
warm and that everything's going
pretty good. I imagine myself on
the Dr. Phil show, with Dr. Phil
himself questioning me.

Dr. Phil: This was a traumatic event and it's not a shock that you're crawling back to him. But you need to look at the *facts*! He *hurt* you and he's going to do it again if you don't back away now. Not responding to his love confessions was the first step, but you need to show him who's the boss here. Can somebody please get her a tissue? We need to talk about the real problems.

I decide I never liked Dr.

Phil and that I find his mustache slightly offensive. And then I kiss him goodnight and head up the stairs, alone.

Jack is already asleep once I get in the room, so I quietly slip off my shoes and curl up in the bed. He always sleeps on the floor when I'm there. I wonder if he sleeps in the bed when I'm not. As soon as my head hits the pillow, he bolts up. Staring at me he asks, "How'd it go?"

"Well, I might be an

official heartbreaker." I mutter into my pillow.

Standing, he gestures, may I? I nod as he sits precariously at the edge of the bed. Rubbing his thumb on my foot, he tells me to explain.

I sigh dramatically.

He starts poking my foot and whines, "Tell me. I want to know everything."

Inhaling deeply, I can feel

tears making their way down my
cheeks. I didn't notice I had
been crying. "Well Jack, here's
the thing. I need to stay as far
away from him as possible. But I
love him, or at least I've done a
great job in fooling myself into
thinking I do. But reminder the
night I went to the hospital?
Those cuts and bruises weren't
from some random guy. Kevin took
me out back and he...hurt me. In
more ways then one. He was drunk,
or at least I think he was. And I
didn't fight back. He hurt me and
he essentially just left me out

there. But you said he brought me to the hospital?"

He nods and mumbles thoughtfully, "Both of us, actually."

"See, that's where I'm getting all mixed up. He saved me, he saved the both of us. And we've been talking this whole time that I haven't been here. But it's that night that just terrifies me in ways I can't explain. I can't eat, I can't sleep, all because of him. But if

it is not love, then what is it?
Call it insanity, hell, call it
Stockholm Syndrome, I don't care.
I need him in my life. And that
haunts me, endlessly."

He stares at his lap,
breathing heavily. Closing his
eyes, he whispers, "God, alright.
I can't sit here and tell you
what to do because based on my
track record, I'd probably be
telling you the wrong thing."
Glancing up at me nervously, he
mumbles, "This might be bad time
to say this, but I got an

apartment back where you live. I can't live here anymore, this city don't want my bones anymore then I do. I hope that's alright.."

My heart skips a beat and I hug him tightly. "This is brilliant, this is so brilliant. We can get back on track again! We can stop drinking and smoking and get healthy, Jack, this is fantastic."

He looks away once again, I can feel his hands shaking.

"Well, uh, that's the thing. I asked Kevin if he wanted to live with me and he said yes."

I can feel my heart drop. Is this what true fear is? No. It'll be fine. No. It won't be fine. I hold my head, I am so dizzy.

"He needs our help," Jack begins, eyeing me warily, "He's as bad off as you and I, it would be cruel of us to just leave him. Besides, we'll be living with this great guy, Richie. I've known him for years but we just started speaking again. I really think it will be the best for all of us."

"We can be cruel." I mutter stubbornly.

He places his fingers under my chin, forcing me to look at him. "Darling, this is the south side of Chicago. It isn't safe here and you know it. He's going to get himself shot, do you want that?" He's whispering furiously now, as if there was someone we didn't want to wake up. I nod,

gesturing that I'm done with the
discussion.

"We'll be there by July."

Part Three

The future has been at war,

but it's on it's way home. It
will be in the door so, so soon.
We just have to make it that far.
Now tell me, is home a place or a
feeling?

Home is the way the light
reflects off the water, creating
daytime stars. Home is the smell
of coffee on your breath, you
have risen before the sun. Home
is the way your favorite song
sounded for the first time. Home
is fireworks in the rain and the
way the ocean looks at dawn.

I have been deemed a
wanderer, but I do believe that
this is what I could learn to
call home. My wanderlust consumes
me, yet I find myself going in an
incessant circle.

I am laying in plush grass,
staring lazily at the water.
Everything is warm and slow, I am
reminded of love and honey. I
hear footsteps behind me but I do
not stir. No, not worth it. Too
comfy.

I can hear Kevin breathing

as he lays down next to me.
Looping my fingers in mine, he
brings my hand up to his mouth,
kissing my knuckles. "I feel that
days like this are little
miracles," He mumbled sleepily,
"Nevermind wine and water, this
is what matters."

I turn away from him,
focusing my gaze on the water
once again. He sighs, almost
inaudibly. He is frustrated
because he is searching for my
heart but all he ever seems to
find is electric fencing and

barbed wire. And to his dismay,
everything soft about me is all
locked up and I have seemed to
have swallowed the key long ago.

Kevin and Jack ended up
moving in about 10 miles away
from me. It's been rather odd,
crocheting them into my life. But
in a good way. I've taken Jack to
my favorite little coffeehouses
and that vintage shop at the end
of the street. Our time together
was always so intimate, the
understanding we have for each
other..magnificent. It was like

reading your favorite book for the 12th time; knowing all the lines to your favorite song. Like looking in the mirror and not hating what's staring back. That is Jack.

Kevin stands up and takes a few steps towards a tree. He is silent, I focus on the water. I compose metaphors in my head. My Golden Tragedy sneaks it's way in there as well. Am I really happy? Is that the purpose of the Golden Tragedy? And in terms of a Golden Tragedy: is it tragically beautiful or beautifully tragic?

Shallow water and sunday mornings. This could almost be it.

I feel a pair of hands grab my waist and lift, I squeal. Suddenly, the water I was just staring at surrounds me. Looking up, I see Kevin standing on the shoreline, grinning proudly. I tilt my head back and laugh. It was one of those laughs that comes from the very depths of you, one of those laughs your

heart saves for moments like
these. Peeling off his shirt, he
comes in after me. Picking me up,
he kisses me on the forehead, I
feel his fingers on my back, each
touch like a promise.

That was the funny thing
about kissing him, it was so much
like drinking salt water. The
more you drink, the more your
thirst increases. It was in this
moment, that I truly believed he
would be the one that would save
me. For we are just humans, if we
can not believe in love, then

what is left for us?

I love him.

Tragically.

Hopelessly.

Tenderly.

Horribly.

It was within his voice that
flowers blossomed, that the
wretched, forgotten souls had
found the promise of a better
tomorrow. It was within this
moment that it occurred to me
that this was as young as I will
ever be, and as old as I have

ever been. What a funny thing to
realize…

I did not see him as the
things he had done, or the things
he had failed to do. That is not
how my eyes wanted to accept him.
Within his velvet mind, was
everything I was not. He was all
those little details you don't
like about yourself, reversed. He
was the cup of black coffee in
the morning that you simply can
not start you day without. He was
words whispered at 3 AM. He was
the sound coming from a winter

day, one where you think
everything is silent for the snow
muffles it all, and yet he was
ringing out.

He pulls away and looks at
me, confused. I tilt my head and
study a hair above his eyebrow.

"What do you see?" He
murmurs.

"Anything I want."

I almost do not recognize
my voice. The words do not sound

like my own, but it was true. It
was all so true.

He nuzzles his nose into my
neck and sighs. He is not
satisfied with my answer. I
understand, for I am the exact
same way. I am overly curious in
till I get the information I
want, except I blow it all away
with a sigh. Looking up at me
once again, he mumbles, "That's
the thing about you. You
fascinate me in the most
dangerous ways. And yet, I could
sleep on your bedroom floor and

feel safer than I ever would in
my own bed."

I make my way towards the
shoreline once again. Crossing my
legs as I sit down in the grass,
I stare longingly at the sunset.
I see him standing in the water
looking at the sky as well. I
never quite understood sunsets, I
felt as if I could never fully
appreciate their beauty. The sky
was painted with vibrant shades
of pink, orange, and red. But
this would be the only time that
this very sunset would decorate

the sky, I would never be able to look at it again like this. I wonder if people realized these things, if they would pause and watch the sunset more often.

But that was my problem, I wanted to keep the sunset. Like you would put a lucky penny in your pocket or press a flower and keep it in a book. I didn't want it to go away, I wanted to sit and stare at it again, when I needed to. To remember.

Another thing I never

understood was, what do sunsets signal, exactly? The end of the day or the beginning of the night? What about sunrises?

I jump when Kevin places his hand on my shoulder. "You looked so distraught, what are you thinking about?"

Blushing, I mumble, "Sunsets."

~

I laid on top of the covers that night. The air was hot and sticky and I loved it. People so often complain about the heat, but a temperature of at least 90 degrees was perfect to me. It was like being wrapped in a giant, volcanic blanket wherever you went. Which is why I was on top of my covers. Normal blankets simply would not do.

I stared at my hands, bending my fingers, clenching my fists. In and out, in and out. The motion was so rhythmic, so simple. The thought of Kevin and mine's earlier confessions haunts my mind. I roll over onto my back, staring intently at the ceiling, as if it could give me all the answers I needed.

My fingertips brushed over my ribs, tapping on them, I could count them all. My hands glided over my sunken in stomach, shriveled from months of restricting, retraining. Palms pressed against my protruding hipbones, I learned to control. I have designed my own catastrophe, perfected my personal hell.

I feel tears burning my eyes from a twisted frustration. I am not skinny enough, I am fat. They say that beauty comes from pain, but what happens when I am numb? What happens when I die from the pain? Is that beautiful? They say beauty comes from ashes, but this scars I have from lighter burns aren't very pretty. They say that beauty comes from inside, all I have is damaged organs, a weeping heart, and a kidney that isn't even mine. Dammit, I couldn't even keep my kidneys in tack.

I bring my hands to my face,
biting my nails. I am shaking, I
am breaking down. Slowly, touch
my cheeks, my nose, I am here. I
cover my ears and try to sleep. I
do not want to hear the sound of
losing the things that I never
found.

But sleep doesn't come, it
never does. I am always the last
one awake, the last light to be
turned off. Confession: I am
afraid of everything except for

the dark.

Relentlessly, my thoughts tug and pull and devour and consume. Consume every inch of me, craving every molecule of my sanity. Sanity, something that I once had but now seems like a part of a sick dream. Dream is all I can do anymore, for reality disappoints me but how can I dream if I can not sleep? Sleep, sleep, yes that is what we need. Need sleep.

I toss and turn and kick and

pull. I can not find the switch
to turn on the light. Perhaps if
I curl up and make myself
smaller, the room will not seem
so empty. The loneliness will not
be so real.

It is tragic for I so often
find myself using humor to cover
up the fact that I want to jump
off of a bridge. I am hiding
behind the tears of a clown. I so
much depend on the mask I have
painted to replace my face, the
vibrant blues and reds distract
everyone from what it really

hides. I crack a joke to flawlessly conceal the gashes hidden under my clothing. A cotton barrier is stronger than anyone ever would have suspected. I laugh too hard so you would notice the vodka scent that lingers behind my gum. I use interesting conversation starters to cover up that I've obviously locked the door but I'm going to do it at least seven more times. I wear layers of stylish clothing to conceal the fact that you can see my bones. You can see my bones. You can see my bones.

The bad news: nothing lasts forever.

The good news: nothing lasts forever.

So I lay in the coat of darkness, drowning in my fears. And you stand but three feet away, shouting at me, to learn how to swim.

This is our final hour, is it not? This is when it all comes unraveling. This is when the

children scream, when the hearts
break. This is when, after
reaching for the bottle of liquor
that I keep on my nightstand, I
croak miserably, that I, have a
problem.

I remember back to the few
hours I spent at the 'recovery
facility' or whatever the
wretched thing has been named. I
think of the grey women and the
pretty corpses. I think of my red
lipstick and my sass. Again, that
same doubt is tugging at the back
of my brain, did I make the right

choice? Walking out? Is this really what is best for me, or should I swallow some *prescribed* happy pills for once?

Maybe I should call Jack.

Maybe I should tell Kevin I love him and make myself believe it.

Maybe I should slit my wrists and bleed out in the bathtub.

Maybe I should get something

to drink.

I think we should get something to drink. What was the quote? Write drunk, edit sober? I want to sleep woozy and wake up even worse. I'll admit it, I'm a complete coward and I'm too afraid to deal with my own problems and the mess that my life has become. In the terms of a Golden Tragedy, this is really tragic, and booze isn't really golden.

I guess it's all downhill

from here.

I think, as I take another
swig from the almost empty
bottle.

I wake up, feeling terrible.
I hate when you don't recall
falling asleep. The last thing I
remember was reaching for the
bottle, but I don't know how many
times I did that. It's like
pacing, you know you're doing it,
you just don't keep track of how
many times you've gone back and
forth. You aren't going anywhere,

but you must keep going. I wake
up and stretch, trying to crack
my back. Of course, it is
unsuccessful and the pounding in
my head is incessant.

I stumble out of bed, having
to steady myself on that same
night stand. I glare at the
bottle as if it was already
staring menacingly. Those last
few drops at the bottom seem to
mock me, laughing at my sloppy
weakness. I run into two other
pieces of furniture and knock
over a lamp all before I open the

damn door. Padding down the
hallway to the bathroom, I catch
a glimpse of myself in the
mirror. Eyes bloodshot, like each
little red river a crack in my
heart. They say you can tell if
someone's lying by looking at
their eyes, I feel as if I have
broken the truth. I have
destroyed it so much that I'm not
sure what is true and what is not
anymore. I stare at the curious
knot of mangled hair piled atop
my head. Must cut off.

Quickly reaching for

foundation, eyeliner, and anything to cover my face and fade the memory of last night, I set to work. Makeup was always something I had this gross, dependant fascination with. It could fix anything from your blemishes to your biggest vices and character flaws! All while each advertisement makes you feel like a deformity! On the subject of bittersweet thoughts, I have discovered that my spirit animal is somewhere dead on the side of the road.

I hear a soft knocking on the front door. I know nobody is home but me, so I drag myself down the stairs to answer it. Jack is looking bleary eyed and terribly lost. "Darling!" I laugh sadly, pulling him inside. Glancing at the window, he mutters something about the sun being too bright at this hour. As if the fact it was noon was something that the world had plotted against him personally.

Plopping himself on the kitchen floor, he looks at me

expectantly. God, he is so cute. I quickly set to making us both two obnoxiously large cups of coffee. Peering into the cup he mumbles, "Black, like the soul. Thank you dearest."

I laugh at that.

Staring absently out the window, he begins, "My thoughts were so loud I couldn't hear my mouth."

Taking a deep breath I whisper, "Forgive me if I don't

talk much, my head makes enough noise."

He laughs at that.

We share this bittersweet happiness between each other over our blatant understanding of just *everything.*

Inhaling deeply, "Darling, I'm falling apart. I told myself I'd stop drinking and here I am last night, strutting out of a coffee shop and strict to the liquor shop. I mean, where have my morals gone? Where is my self control! I just felt so upset over everything. It was as if the weight of the world was on my shoulders and I was suffocating. Yet not a single soul, out of the whatever billion people, offered to help. And I was just so sad."

I nodded, thinking about my own relapse. I suppose that's what it felt like, but addiction really just comes crawling at the door and when you tell it no, it gnaws on the handle. I saw a quote once that really explained everything. It was, "The mind of the addict is cunning enough to convince the body it is not dying. Houdini doesn't have shit on an addict."

Magic? maybe.

Dying? perhaps.

Living? no.

This ceaseless temptation, it aches inside of you, yet no amount of liquor persuades it to stop crying out to me.

Glancing at the calendar, I
discover what day it is. My
sister, the one I had briefly
mentioned, was coming home today.
My family and I were going to
meet her in the airport. She was
like a branch that had fallen. It
tries to be drafted to a
different family tree, but ends
up mixed into a drink: two parts
rejection, three parts sadness.

I suppose her and I had been
the black uh, swans of the
family. See, we didn't look like

anyone else, but we resembled each other. We were both complex, complicated, misunderstood. She speaks too much, I speak too little. We are not black and white from each other, simply different shades of grey. I do not understand her, she can not comprehend me. I do not blame her for this is a voluptuous task that I highly caution anyone on undertaking. You will end up frustrated and very, very sad. So we bonded on our differences.

I listen to classical music,

she listens to death metal.

I whisper, she screams.

I go left, she goes right.

But we both aren't picky
about whether it is tea or
coffee, as long as it's warm and
caffeinated.

Small rodents are adorable,
so we don't eat them. Or any
other animals, for that matter.

It is little agreements like

this that have kept us close, the timeless ones. That was all we had. But here we were, and she was coming back to me. I have not seen her in so long. My stomach knots itself in protest to literally everything.

After a long stretch of mutual silence, Jack and I stand up at the same time. Glancing over at me, he smiles sadly. "It is a big day for you." He declares. I feel as if he was going to say something after that, but his words fall flat and

he makes his way towards the
door, promising he'll call and
wishing me the best of luck.

If I have learned everything
in all of my years, luck has
nothing to do with fate.

But it was sweet of him to
say, anyway.

The hours are slow, but this
goes without saying. I pace, I
bite my nails, I wring my hands.
We proceed to the airport as if
we were going to a funeral. Tell

me, is this the beginning of the
end, or merely the end of the
beginning?

I wait, anxiously. I stare
at each figure walking by,
searching their faces for some
sort of clue to where she is. I
feel as if I have lost her, more
than ever before, in these very
moments.

But she walks, she runs.

She is a black figure, a
large winter coat in the middle

of July. She is skin and bones, she is fragile, she is broken. She is a flower that had simply forgotten to be watered, let me find the can and a vase. No, not a vase, we can not confine her. Let us plant her outside. Let me fix her.

I hug her and fear that I will break her.

I hug her and fear that she will lift up my sleeves and see the nights in which she could not guide me, the years that she missed.

I hug her and fear that she
will turn around and walk back
towards the plane.

She hugs people like she can
never hug them again. It is those
rib-crushing, lung-constricting
types of hugs.

I translate the phrase 'she
is crying' into French behind my
eyelids.

We all eventually make our
way back to the car, the silence

is deafening. Saying hello only takes so long. We all sit and wonder together, where do we go from here? She watches me, intently. A bitter part of me wants her to stop staring at me, but I simply look forward. My mom is rambling off on how we *missed her* and how we're *so happy to have her home*. I gag.

This is the exact woman who gossips about her children, peering at an uninterested husband over a glass of wine.

Because apparently you're still a lady if what drunkens you is worth more than twenty dollars.

Through wine soaked lips, I have listened to her scream, rant, blame, and ramble about this very same person. There is nothing that I hate more than two faced people.

I could never understand how cheerleaders could screw the entire football team on Saturday night and then be claimed virginal goddesses on Sunday morning. I have decided this is the same sort of phenomenon.

Peering out the window, I remember my mom telling me how she was a cheerleader. And Homecoming Queen. And a straight A student. And class president. And a model. And a perfect small town southern bell.

Maybe she's simply frustrated now that she's discovered that that type of perfection expires.

So she sits and smiles
fakely at the sight of her *two
beautiful daughters who are such
a blessing and she wouldn't know
what to do without.*

She asks for our love and
attention like a small child
would beg for a piece of candy at
a grocery store.

She's never going to get it
and it doesn't really matter
anyway.

We make our way into the house. If there are more people in it than this morning, why does it seem emptier than before?

I glance around, taking in the familiar decor once more. We have one of those overly clean houses, like something you would find out of a magazine. People always gasp in awe when they walk in and say something along the lines of: *OMG people actually like, live here?*

Plot twist: they don't.

I giggle quietly and everyone's eyes shoot towards me. Sorry.

Deciding that I played my part well enough, I retreat upstairs.

I'd be shocked if they couldn't make it an hour without biting each other's heads off, not with her just coming back, so my 'protecting duties' are momentarily on hold. See that's one thing I'm good at- fighting.

I'm stubborn and generally surrounded by people that give up easily.

My life's a mess and I hate my family a good 99.999% of the time- but I'm stubborn! Praise the Lord for my good fortune. I guess.

I sit on my bed and calmly eavesdrop. I devise a movie script in my head for the situation downstairs.

The character, 'Mom':

Pretending to be humble and slightly nervous, she throws herself into a down to earth, Martha Stewart like ego. She putters around the kitchen because there is 'so much work to be done' and she must conserve her housewife image, which she pretends to hate but does everything in her power to conserve and protect. Must ask if anyone wants something to drink *at least* 12 times. Add another 15 for the topic of eating.

The character, 'Dad': Be

gruff, but the all-american family guy. Act as if you and the eldest daughter have some sort of deep understanding of one another. Ask questions you already know the answer to. After quickly running out of things to say, resort to scrolling through the mass of opened junk mail on your e-mail. Feel free to occasionally mumble irrelevant things to yourself, as if your work is more important than your family. Because in your eyes, money is love, happiness, and the only thing of value.

The character, 'sister':
Give short, quick, yet honest
responses to all awkward
questions. Adjusting your jacket,
you don't want to take it off
because *it's freezing in here,*
but you do anyway because that's
polite. Resembling something like
a deer wandering to cross the
street or not, gently make your
way upstairs in hopes of talking
to your sister.

The character, 'me': Mumble
most, if not all of your

responses, no one is listening anyway. Sit silently in your room, pretending and hoping that you don't exist. Act pleasantly surprised when you hear the knock on your door. When in all reality, your heart dropped when you heard her footsteps coming towards the stairs.

My sister and I perch awkwardly on the edge of my bed. The room has changed significantly since she was last here. It's only been a good three years. What was once cluttered and awkward, is now cluttered, awkward, and mainly black. No, I am not following in her footsteps, for I am not her. Black is not a lifestyle, it is a color and it is sophisticated, classy, and timeless. I will not be dying my hair black, piercing my everything, wearing band shirts, and talking incessantly about how no one 'gets me' anytime soon.

It is just one more thing we don't have in common.

She's slightly emotional and fragile. I have perfected the art of being submissive, apathetic, and heartless. She honestly reminds me of myself before I fell apart. She has this innocence to her, no matter what.

I have a fascination with people like this. See, I believe that people's souls are crystal clear and so white when we are born. But somewhere in between innocence and..the rest of everything, this purity is damaged. Of course it is. It is as if everything bad thing you have ever done, leaves little fingerprints on your soul. The amount of dirt on your soul affects the words that come out of your mouth and the thoughts that enter your brain. And yet, there are these people who have fingerprints on their soul, but they have this light to them.

Oh, I love exceptions.

And so she speaks to me, trying to dive into the

relationship we had three years ago. How does one casually fill her in on *three years* of events? I feel like I should have a worksheet, like you get on the first day of school.

I imagine standing up to introduce myself: Hello, sister. I enjoy classical music and play cello in till my fingers bleed. I don't talk a lot because I feel like people too often hear, but don't listen. I get really anxious and I haven't really slept in a few days to be

perfectly honest. And to be even
more frank with you, this whole
thing stresses me out, so don't
feel offended when you ask me a
question and I don't respond.
Trust me, it's not you, it's me.

Instead, I sit and try to
tell her about school. As if
that's what's important. It's all
so strange, like stumbling upon a
box of childhood artifacts. They
were once so important to you,
but you're different now. So you
sit and hold them awkwardly,
telling yourself that it's the

right thing to do. When in all
reality, you're still a scared
little kid, but now you're forced
to put on your grown up shoes and
trudge on through everything.

Sensing that my guards up,
she decides to disregard it
entirely. She digs deeper,
pressing, pressing, *what is
wrong*. I think that she realizes
the gash that her not being here
has made on everything. But I
will not sit here and tell you
that I didn't cry for months,
curled up with the letter she

left me like a broken record. I
will not sit here and tell you
that I did not have a little-girl
like happiness when I found out
that I'd see her again. I will
not sit here and tell you that a
day passed without me worrying
about her because then I would be
lying. I have done that enough
already.

So taking a deep breath, I
begin to talk.

"I feel lost inside myself,"
I begin, "There are words that I

need to say, and people that I
need to say them to- people I'm
willing to say them to. But, they
get caught in my throat and to
this day they are just bunched
there, like a clogged drain. That
is my body, a clogged drain of
words unsaid. I am splitting at
the seams, my skin rips away at
itself at the fault of my own
hand and I'm sorry. I'm so so
sorry."

I didn't know how to tell
you that I missed you so I carved
the feeling of it into my skin.

Here, I still have the scars for last week, last month, last year. My lumpy flesh depicts a story in a language of memories that only I can fully understand. Every perfectly parallel mark is a fingerprint on my soul. Please let me explain, I am hurting inside but when that happens I have this horrible habit of injuring my outside as well. It's not my fault, I'm strange, I'm deformed.

My throat gets that closed up feeling and my eyes get that

awkward burning sensation and now
the tears are running down my
cheeks and now she's putting her
arms around me.

I am eight years old again.

Mom and dad are fighting
again, I sit at the end of the
vastly long table. It seems to
stretch on forever; when in all
reality it is a mere few inches
separating me from them. Faces
red and constricted, my parents
turn away from me, towards my
sister at the opposite end. I

watch her grow frustrated, she is crying. Yelling words that don't make sense to me, that don't make sense to her, she is a rabbit trying to defend herself against a wolf. There is no chance, no other options. She stands up, pushing the chair over defiantly and scurries towards the stairs. But she is trapped.

She is

Hands to arm, forced to the floor.

Bruised skin, I have learned

that memories are purple.

Scarred flesh, for she is
bound to never forgetting this
night.

Scraped, as if from rope,
constricting her to the family.

The burden of this household
that will follow her for
eternity.

Salty tears and screaming
lips.

A tornado of betrayal and
confusion,

A hurricane of regret.

Overly polite dinner
conversation gone wrong.

Dents in our wooden floors
that we could never polish over.

A scene that will play
behind my eyelids for years to
come.

I shut my eyes in case she
can read my thoughts. But even
then, something tells me that she
knows.

I am turning and leaving and
walking downstairs. My thoughts
are closing in with hands around
my neck and I can not breath.
Please do not touch me, do not
hold me, do not tell me you love

me because I might make the fatal
mistake of believing that it is
true.

You know, speaking comes
from instinct. Silence comes from
understanding. Do not blame me
for when I chose to not use my
words, they are simply not
enough.

My father comes upstairs,
stopping us in the hallway. "I
was thinking it was time to take
her home." He states politely,
blatantly ignoring the tears on

my cheeks.

"Oh."

And just like that, it is
over. Everything was so much like
that moment when you wake up from
a nightmare. You are sweaty,
shaking, and clutching that old
pillow that you don't recall the
last time you washed. But it's
over. Are you relieved? Or
disappointed because you don't
know how the story ends? As I
walk back to my room, I almost
expect her to be sitting there,

just as she was minutes before.
But just like how the monster is
actually not inside of the
closet, I am alone again.

Alone, alone, alone. The
word echoes between the walls,
embedding itself in the threads
of my sheets. Alone, alone,
alone. My nails dig and claw at
my flesh, searching for something
more than this. There has to be
something more. I can not be
miserable forever.

But I am such

a...procrastinator when it comes to myself. I feel like I should make a bunch of inspiration post it notes and a list of goals and tape them around my house. But that just isn't me. So, to be frank, I'm going to lie to myself a little bit more, cut a little deeper, eat a little less, become a little wiser.

So I sit down and I write. I write in till it doesn't hurt. I write in till my hand and my heart are numb. Sitting back, I stare at the ink covered paper.

Examining the evidence, this is
what I read:

Pierce my sides and watch me bleed out,
All the reasons on why you deserve *one
more chance.*

See, I treated you like you were
The last oxygen molecule in a gas chamber-
Oh, I was good to you.

I traded integrity for security and called it
love.

You would ask me how I got these scars,
I'd tell you I had swallowed my pride
And it clawed it's way out of my mouth;
That I had ripped every last piece of you out
of my smile.

But it wasn't enough so you loved work
more than me,

Money more than me,
Her more than me,
And I loved you, *more than me.*

So you begged for plastic perfection,
Hidden in temptations, inches away from
your face,
I could *feel* the lies when you said the
wretched words,
"You are so beautiful."

I would tie you up to a nightmare and
auction you off,
To the memories that so often keep me from
sleeping.

For there is nothing logical about cutting off
The most fragile parts of you and placing
them
In hands that tremble and shake-
Let me offer you what little wisdom I
possess,
They will be dropped.

Exhale. There is blood on the page but nonetheless I am still somewhat proud.

Inhale. We are starting to scrape out the jumbled words that have been stuck in my body for so long

Exhale. This is just the beginning.

Inhale. I think of my heart like an overgrown bush. I am taking a rake and scraping out all of the shit that's piled up inside of it. Yes, the maggots are nasty and my blisters hurt but we can't stop now. Not in till the leaves turn towards the light, creating oxygen for me to breath in.

Exhale. Exhale the oxygen, speak. I have a voice. I do not need to use it for my words are on paper but *I have a voice*.

I am hyperventilating.

No more writing for tonight.
But this is a good start.
Glancing down at my phone, it
whines at me. 6 text messages and
2 missed calls. Kevin is worried.
My chest does that weird thing
where it clenches up and your
heart skips a beat. I worry that
I am having a heart attack.
Pausing only a minute to decide
whether or not heart attacks are
bad, I drop the silent debate
with myself and call him.

His voices rings through
like liquid gold. "Angel, are you
alright?"

And just like that the
butterflys fly away. My nerves
loosen their forever tightening
grip on my chest; my heart stops
attacking itself. My voice
answers clear, smooth. "Yes, I'm

alright. Let me tell you about what happened today." And just like that I start retelling the story of my day and it is so simple, so easy. I don't stumble over my words or question myself. I just tell.

This sort of thing is sort of a big deal for people like me. So often I have longed to rip the stitching that binds my lips together, let the words flow free. But it can not be that simple, for all of the things unsaid are clogged in my throat, making it disgusting and swollen. Sometimes I believe that it is better they remain there. Let the house rot so no one else will ruin it further.

He is laughing.

"Angel, you stopped in the middle of your sentence again."

Blushing madly, I mutter

about how I need to stop doing
that.

So badly, I need to fit into
his world, just as the frame of
my body needs to fit in his arms,
like pieces in a puzzle. He makes
me feel as if there was nothing
ever missing. As if he was never
far away, but just always out of
reach...

I wake up with my phone
still clutched in my hand. It is
making noises at me again. Jack
is reminding me that I have yet
another shoot today. Rolling out
of bed, I try and shake the bad
memories as if it could go away
in an hours time like my
grogginess.

He picks me up in an old,
black car. It smells like
cigarettes and film litters the
floor. Informing me that the car
is Richie's, I realize I have yet

to meet him. I have heard so many
things that involve him, but
nothing *about* him. I need to
thank him for everything he has
done, I need to give this face a
name. I will forever feel
incomplete if I do not. I try to
shake that as well.

We eventually arrive at a
group of apartment buildings,
somewhere downtown. Knocking on a
stained door, a hooded man opens
it reluctantly. Gathering my
strength, I extend my hand. He
does not take it. He stares and
stares at me, into me. It was the
type of stare that would not make
you self conscious of your
appearance, but of your thoughts
and of your heart. Quickly
growing uncomfortable, Jack grips
my arm and gathers me into his
jacket.
Rushing me away, he mumbles,
"Wrong place."

We do not try and search for

where we should have been.

I leave him, I do not invite him in. As strange as it might sound, I could not shake the feeling I got back there. It feels as if I am being watched but no one is around. It is a type of paranoia that seeps into the cracks and crevices of your being.

I stare out my window, searching for something, someone. But the street remains empty. The only movement is the falling leaves, the rustling of now bare branches. Pulling my sweater over my shoulders, I know that winter will be here soon.

~

The past few weeks have been mostly uneventful. Just the typical preparations for the holidays and getting settled in with the concept of winter. It is

Christmas Eve and Kevin is pinching my cheeks. Leaning down, he whispers into my ear, "I have beautiful things to give you."

Giggling, I playfully swat at his arm. "You didn't need to get me anything, silly!" I cover up the fact that I had his gift picked out weeks ago, after searching for the perfect thing. It was a ring, custom made with an engraving of my handwriting which read, *everything*. I was ridiculously proud of it.

We were cuddled up under a blanket next to the fireplace and he had his fingers tangled in my hair. The tree was lit so warmly, all the ornaments looked like little treasures. I could stare at it for hours. I was so giddy with everything. The air around me had this wonderful aroma of Kevin's cologne, evergreens, and belonging. It was all so *right*, as if us sitting next to each other, quietly blushing in anticipation for tomorrow, was exactly what we were created to do.

He rubs his thumb over the small tracks of uneven skin on my right forearm. They serve as silent reminders of the night he first laid his hands on me. Distant warnings of what he was capable of. He quickly moves down to my wrist and gently wraps his hand around it. We are both shaking.

Neither of us say anything about it. The memory was painful and I didn't want to be reminded of it. I didn't want to admit that I had blindly continued on into this huge mess of depending on him, knowing what he had done to me and that he could do it again. I needed him.

So we sit by the fire in silence for a bit more. But it

was getting late and the same, warm excitement for the following day returned. "You nervous?" He mumbles into my hair.

Nodding, I smile. "You have to like it. Please like it. Please love it. I'll be a mess if you don't."

Sighing happily, he looks at our hands, clasped tightly together. "I love you." He murmurs.

He stands and lets my hand fall. Kissing the top of my head, he departs. Before he closes the door, he looks back at me. I smile and wave.

I kept my phone by my bedside, just in case he called to say good night. But I fell asleep soon after he left.

The loud, obnoxious ringtone

pulls me from my sleep. I
scramble to answer the call in
time. Assuming it was Kevin, I
mumbled sleepily, "Hello my love,
I've missed you."

But there is no response.
Checking the screen, I see that
it was indeed Kevin I was talking
to. "Kevin?" I ask hesitantly.

He chokes out a very
restrained sob. But it soon pours
out from him. I can tell he isn't
holding the phone to his ear, he
sounds distant. He apologizes
over and over again.

"Kevin, what's wrong? What
happened? Are you hurt?"

No response.

"Kevin please talk to me,
you're scaring me."

Still no response, he continues to apologize.

"Don't do this. Please don't do this."

I can feel myself growing frantic, tears threaten to pour down my cheeks.

"I'm coming over." I announce.

There was something so unnerving in the quiet that followed.

Pulling on my boots, I glance at the clock and notice it's only a little after six. He would never call at this hour unless something was really wrong. My parents spent the holiday with some friends, they wouldn't be back for a couple of days. I didn't have to worry about waking anyone up as I dashed down the stairs.

The frigid air bit at my exposed arms and legs. I cursed myself for not bringing a jacket. I picked up the pace to a jog, the house was about eight miles away. I could do it as long as I paced myself. But as the seconds went by, my anxiety built. I am sprinting.

Tearing down the familiar roads, the pavement seems to be mocking me. My breathing becomes frantic and strained.
I can hear the voice in my head telling me I was weak, that I was useless. I press on.

I pass a house with lights on. Glancing into the windows, I see two tired parents smiling at their young children as they unwrap gifts by a tree. Tears sting my eyes.

Why could that not be me?

Why do I not have any memories like that? Why was I not celebrating this holiday with my loved ones, my parents? I run faster.

My lungs feel as if they are collapsing, I am no longer cold. I am numb. The rhythmic slapping of my boots on the pavement is what I focus my attention on. I am so close.

Seeing the familiar driveway, I tear forward and rip open the front door. Standing in the small foyer, I start yelling his name. I hear him crying.

I bolt towards his bedroom, slipping on the steps. And then I hear it.

Gunshot. Like blowing out a candle, the house grows silent like a room would go dark.

I am screaming.

I am running.
I am not fast enough.
Too late, too late.

He is on the ground, why is
he not moving? Why is he not
breathing?

A mass of red stains his
skin, I grab his body. Why is he
not moving. Why isn't he smiling.
It's Christmas. Why isn't he
happy. Why aren't we like the
family in the window. Why isn't
he smiling.

My hands are shaking, like
an almost complete painting, you
can hardly see the color of my
skin through the mess. I am
holding him so tightly, as if I
could glue all of his broken
pieces back together. I am
clutching his name with such a
severity that it turns to dust.

I can not stop screaming.

My body is an earthquake
with every sob that escapes my
lips. I can not see past the
tears so I close my eyes and I
just hold him. I can not tell if
I had stopped screaming.

There was a train, derailing
itself and wreaking havoc on my
sanity. I can feel every part of
myself that was once so whole and
so pure, collapsing in on itself.
All that was left of me was a
wretched, twisted lie.

When something like this
happens, a part of you snaps and
breaks. You can never repair it.
Trust me, I've tried. I could
physically feel my heart snapping
in two; rupturing, becoming a
pulpy mess and dying. It was as
if we had ended our lives
together. It was as if I wasn't
breathing, as if my heart wasn't

beating. There was no reason that I could see for it to continue on.

I feel hands grabbing onto my waist and I lash out. I hit as hard as I can, I dig my nails into their flesh. I can hear the man yelling, begging me to stop. I do not stop, I was going to protect Kevin, I promised I always would. He could not take him away from me.

Opening my eyes, I see a pair of tear filled eyes staring at me. I recognize them and they are afraid. It is Jack.

"You have to let go." He whispers.

I can not.

I am a bloody mess and his body is cold but I can not. My

hands are shaking from how hard I am gripping him but I can not.

I shake my head and I cry.

I feel him scooping us both up, I can feel Kevin's dead weight against me. My vision clouds and I faint.

I wake up on a bed.
Sitting up, I try to balance myself. I am still covered in dried blood. I see across the hallway that the door to Kevin's room is closed. I can hear two hushed voices coming from the lower level. I slowly try to make my way down the stairs.

Peering past a wall, I see Jack and another guy sitting at a table. They both have their head in their hands. Tapping on the wall, I mumble hello. Jack immediately bolts up and comes

over to hug me. I can feel him
crying. He reluctantly lets go,
allowing me to shake hands with
the one who introduces himself to
me as Richie. He is tall with an
extremely noticeable pink, fleshy
scar on his right cheek.

We all don't really say
much. Richie offers me some cold
coffee and we mutually sit in
silence. After a couple hours,
they drive me home, saying we'll
see each other again soon, under
better circumstances.

The walls around me seemed
so different, yet I knew they had
remained exactly the same. I was
the only one who had changed. I
trudge up the stairs to take a
much needed shower. Stripping
down, I stare at my blood covered
arms. That's when it hits me. He
isn't coming back. Stepping into
the shower, the hot water burns
my skin and I don't care- he
isn't coming back. Watching the

rose red flow down the drain- he isn't coming back. Scrubbing off every part of him- he isn't coming back.

Stepping out, I look in the mirror once again. My skin is still red, but not from blood. It is burned. Slowly, slowly, I reach for my knees and pull myself down. I cry again. I cry about him. I cry about how much everything hurts. I cry about the number on the scale. I cry about lost love. I cry about the scars on my body. But most of all, I cry about what a damn mess I am. *I cry.*

I guess that's the best way to explain it. That's what it's like, reaching your breaking point. It was the last straw. Suddenly, I was forced to realize everything that was wrong. Forced to say that I was not okay. Suddenly, you aren't' crying about what had just happened, you

are crying about everything. For
all the times that you couldn't
let yourself cry, those tears
don't go away. They wait and they
are all rushing back right at
that moment, screaming, hello,
you are not okay.

Part Three

I went to his burial. There were three of us. Three. Jack, Richie, and myself. That hit me like a ton of bricks. He always seemed so big, so bright. The type of person who would have people cross oceans and deserts for, just to pay their respects. But there we were, standing in the snow, feeling pitiful.

We buried him at that lake where Jack had first taken me,

all those months ago. Right down
next to the water.

Neither of them looked like
they were going to speak, which
was okay because sometimes
silence is the best thing you
have to offer.

I decided that for once in
my life, I was not going to
remain quiet. Breathing deeply, I
began.

"I don't know you. I guess I
never have. But you were the best
question I've ever had. Still
are...I have this box of
butterflies though, I took them
out of my stomach. Most of them
are still alive. For you, I will
set them free. I can only hope
that they somehow make their way
to you. They were always yours,
anyway."

I knew he wasn't there,
listening. But a part of me will

always think that he was. That same part of me believes that those butterflies did make their way back to him. And I guess that's all I'll ever be able to do, all anyone can ever do. Because the world is large, the people are confusing, but you have to believe in those butterflies. You have to keep going.

It was such a beautiful war. Still is.

A Word

I suppose I have some explaining to do. Some of you might have realized that the main character was never given a name. This story has bits and pieces of

many people, including myself.
This story is one giant puzzle,
composed of the nights I have
spent talking to these people.
I'd like to thank them for
telling me. I know how hard that
can be. But the idea was, that
someone out there could relate to
this. Maybe not all of it. But
even just a little bit, and find
comfort in that and discover that
they are not alone and they never
will be. She was not given a name
because she is yours to keep.

Another aspect behind this
book was to raise awareness, of
course. Awareness of not just the
fact that things like eating
disorders and self harm exist,
but for those of us who have not
experienced them, to better
understand what it's like.

Honestly, this is the first
book I've written. I had things
to say and I said them. I thank
you for making it this far. But
my words, they have not run dry
yet.

Speaking of words, I do believe a few thank yous are in order. To the people who let their lives intertwine with my own, thank you for listening, for speaking, and for dealing with my madness. I'm not sure if there is a method to it.Thank you to Milon, also for listening, even when I am not speaking. I'd also like to thank my sister. You inspire me in ways that I can never describe, you are the only one who is never failing to notice me, and you give me the hope to believe in things that I told myself to never acknowledge as existing. I am eternally grateful for you. And for my 7th grade English teacher, you are the one who started all of this. Thank you.

Made in the USA
Lexington, KY
14 January 2014